VERY
SMALL
CAFÉS
& RESTAURANTS

**LAURENCE KING**

Published in 2011 by Laurence King Publishing Ltd
361–373 City Road
London EC1V 1LR
Tel: +44 (0)20 7841 6900
Fax: +44 (0)20 7841 6910
E-mail: enquiries@laurenceking.com
www.laurenceking.com

405900

This book was produced by Laurence King Publishing Ltd, London

A catalogue record for this book is available from the British Library

ISBN: 978 1 85669 731 6

Designed by hoopdesign.co.uk

Printed in China

# VERY
# SMALL
# CAFÉS
# & RESTAURANTS

## JOHN
## STONES

LAURENCE
KING
PUBLISHING

# CONTENTS

INTRODUCTION 8

## CAFÉS AND DELICATESSENS

**EAST BEACH CAFÉ** Design: Thomas Heatherwick, Littlehampton, UK 24

**THE ROYAL CAFÉ** Design: Lo Østergaard and Rud Christiansen, Copenhagen, Denmark 30

**COSO CAFÉ** Design: Francesco Moncada, Massimo Tepedino, Ornella Gasbarro, Palermo, Italy 36

**ESPRESSO *K** Design: 2012 Architecten, Delft, Netherlands 42

**JOHN STREET TEA AND WINE** Design: David Collins Studio, Kilkenny, Ireland 46

**THE DEPTFORD PROJECT** Design: Studio Myerscough, London, UK 52

**REPÚBLICA CAFÉ** Design: Ernesto de Ceano and DCD Interiorismo, Seville, Spain 58

**ILLY PUSH BUTTON CAFÉ** Design: Adam Kalkin, Venice, Italy 62

**THE PLANT CAFÉ ORGANIC** Design: CCS Architecture, San Francisco, USA 66

**SILVER CAFÉ** Design: ARCA, Morecambe, UK 70

## PIZZERIAS, PASTA RESTAURANTS AND TAPAS BARS

**PIZZA BAR** Design: Al Taglio, Parallel Design, New York, USA 78

**ESTADO PURO** Design: James & Mau, Madrid, Spain 84

**PIZZA PEREZ** Design: Francesco Moncada, Syracuse, Italy 90

**LA CASA AZUL** Design: Herme Ciscar and Mónica García, Valencia, Spain 96

**JULIA'S PASTA** Design: Merkx+Girod, Amsterdam, Netherlands 102

## SUSHI AND NOODLE BARS

**CHA CHA MOON** Design: Kengo Kuma & Associates, London, UK 108

**WAKU-WAKU** Design: Ippolito Fleitz Group, Hamburg, Germany 114

**ITSU** Design: Afroditi Krassa, London, UK 118

## ICE CREAM PARLOURS AND YOGURT BARS

FROLICK   Design: Asylum, Singapore — 124

TANGYSWEET   Design: Kube Architecture, Washington, DC, USA — 130

SNOG   Design: Cinimod Studio and Ico Design, London, UK — 136

RONO ICE CREAM   Design: Hiroyuki Miyake, Aichi, Japan — 142

## BURGER BARS, CAFETERIAS AND OTHER SMALL RESTAURANTS

McDONALD'S   Design: McDonald's Europe and Philippe Avanzi, Atelier Archange, across Europe — 150

KIRSCHGARTEN CAFETERIA   Design: HHF Architects, Basel, Switzerland — 156

LITTLE CHEF   Design: Ab Rogers, Kettering, UK — 162

RESTAURANT 51   Design: Mut-Architecture and Le Potager Design, Paris, France — 166

CAMPER FOODBALL   Design: Martí Guixé, Barcelona, Spain — 172

PLUK   Design: Tjep., Haarlem, Netherlands — 176

BLOOM IN THE PARK   Design: Jonas Lindvall and Mikael Ling, Lindvall A&D, Malmö, Sweden — 180

SWEETGREEN   Design: Core, Bethesda, USA — 186

BOOLEAN   Design: Torafu Architects, Toyko, Japan — 192

FISH 349   Design: Terroir, Hobart, Tasmania, Australia — 196

BRGR   Design: Rockwell Group, New York, USA — 202

PROEF   Design: Marije Vogelzang, Amsterdam, Netherlands — 208

BLOSSOM   Design: Ryuji Nakamura, Nagano, Japan — 214

## CONFECTIONERY RESTAURANTS

100%CHOCOLATECAFÉ   Design: Wonderwall, Tokyo, Japan — 220

KARA'S CUPCAKES   Design: Montalba Architects, San Francisco, USA — 224

ARTISAN DU CHOCOLAT   Design: Lens°Ass Architecten, London, UK — 230

CANDY RESTAURANT   Design: Martí Guixé, Tokyo, Japan — 236

CHOCOLATE RESEARCH FACILITY   Design: Asylum, Singapore — 242

PROJECT CREDITS — 248

INDEX — 251

PICTURE CREDITS AND ACKNOWLEDGEMENTS — 255

CAR HERE
SOCONY
EAT
EAT PENN DINER
PARKING
50¢
MOBILGAS
6
93
Penn Diner
HOME COOKING
BEER

INTRODUCTION

1

**A YOUNG RUSSIAN TUCKS** into a Big Mac that promises a first taste of American consumerism, with its squeaky plastic packaging and brash graphics. Meanwhile an elderly man whiles away the day with a newspaper in the genteel surroundings of the 18th century Caffè Florian in Venice. These are the two ends of a continuum in which the cafés and small restaurants of this book are to be found.

Small cafés and restaurants have a rich cultural history – evocative not only of particular cultures but of particular moments in time, whether it be 1950s America or fin-de-siècle Vienna. They are important spaces that frame social rituals, where the presence of food can seem almost incidental; they are places to hang out, whether for bored teenagers, Parisian intellectuals, busy mums taking a break from shopping, office workers on their lunch hour or the kind of solitary figure painted by Edward Hopper.

Few things define our respective national identities as much as the way in which we snack. Venues such as tea houses, sausage stands, espresso bars, fish and chip shops and coffee houses are intimately tied up with their countries of origin. This is even more evident when it comes to the food itself: bento, hotdogs, hamburgers, pizza, pommes frites,

2

3

falafel, kebabs, tapas, sandwiches, churros, tacos, sushi, croque-monsieur – the list is almost endless.

There is a customary distinction between high- and low-brow eateries, with places like Venice's Caffè Florian or the Café Schwarzenberg in Vienna featuring somewhere near the top and fast food joints such as MacDonald's being somewhere near the bottom. These are distinctions based on social prestige, quality of food and so on, and are not the concern of this book. Both kinds of venue offer informal food in a social environment, and their design brief is conceptually similar. The extensive and convincing critiques of 'junk food' (and the growing support for 'slow food') are, of course, important, but the moral and health differences between a calorie-laden slice of gateau with coffee that has been sourced for taste rather than ethics in a prestigious coffee house and a quick burger and fries in a chain burger bar may be moot. Similarly, the quality of the design of the venues may not be so very different.

When it comes to the design of fast food restaurants and cafés, it is often the view that retro is good, and contemporary is bad. The extravagant, streamlined forms, neon lights and shiny surfaces of American fast food

4

5

5 A riot of fast food brands
   competing for attention at the
   entrance to a mall in Las Vegas.

6 The evocative golden arches of a
   vintage McDonald's in Lexington,
   Kentucky, photographed in 1981.

6

restaurants of the mid 20th century are the subject of
countless homages, in film, photography and pop videos.
The tackiness of the English 'greasy spoon' – the cheap
café serving simple 'greasy' food – is now fetishised
and savoured, for example in the work of Martin Parr, a
photographer who has put particular care into documenting
fast food. Food snobbism – with or without the social and
environmental critique that has build up around fast food
– has tended to blind people to the significant and wide
ranging design sophistication that goes with the average
fast food outlet. From the presentation of the food itself to
the crockery, from the graphics to the interior, everything is
given very careful consideration.

It is significant that one of the most comprehensive and
widely read critiques of fast food, Eric Schlosser's *Fast Food
Nation*, first published in 2001, is careful not to dismiss the
aesthetics and design of the emerging chains but to describe
their power. Recounting the way in which McDonald's
established its unified face to the world in the 1960s, tearing
down the original restaurants put in place by founders
Richard and Maurice McDonald (who had originally worked
as film set builders before branching out into fast food),

Schlosser writes:

'The distinctive architecture of each chain became
its packaging, as strictly protected by copyright
laws as the designs on a box of soap. The McDonald's
Corporation led the way in the standardization of
America's retail environments, rigorously controlling
the appearance of its restaurants inside and out.'

From traditional coffee house to hamburger joints, informal
eateries conceal a fascinating yet little acknowledged
archaeology of the present. Often the national identity
of a food or environment involves a complex game of
transplantation – the 'hamburger' or 'frankfurter' in the USA,
the Viennese café serving 'Turkish' coffee and the Tandoori
restaurant in Britain all point to different cultures and yet
also manage to seem intrinsic to their new home. New
foods are introduced, often by immigrants, and a particular
stylized environment then evolves, melding aspects of the
new and old that packages up a taster of another culture.

As such, small cafés and restaurants are some of the
most eloquent expressions of a continual process of cultural

7

7 The exquisite interior of a subterranean tea room in the Vakil Bazaar, part of the historic centre of the Iranian city of Shiraz.

8 A mid 19th century painting of a coffee house in Constantinople by Amadeo Preziosi, a Maltese nobleman whose Orientalist watercolours of everyday Turkish life were very popular in Europe.

8

9

9 View out of the window of a
typical fish and chip restaurant
in the seaside resort town of
Blackpool in the north of England.

10 A period image of the Willow
Grove Diner in Pennsylvania
from around 1948. Typically
located at the junction of major
routes, its interior form and
layout is heavily derived from
that of railway diners.

exchange. Take the coffee house, probably the best known example. Already documented in Turkey and Arabia in the 16th century, coffee houses were introduced to Europe from the Muslim world through commerce with the east-facing port of Venice, and coffee crazes gripped nations in different and lasting ways.

When Vienna, under siege from the Turks in 1683, managed to regain its liberty, mythology has it that a single sack of coffee beans was left behind, sparking an enduring obsession not only with coffee but with the accompanying social rituals. But rather than seeing a man smoking a hookah pipe you are more likely to see a middle-aged lady with her shopping bags, though it is usually still possible to order 'Turkish' coffee stewed in a small brass pot. More recently, the opening of the first McDonald's in Moscow in 1990 was an event of enormous symbolic importance, reported the world over, emblematic of the changes that would sweep Soviet Russia away.

While the cultural exchanges and what we now understand as multiculturalism strongly inform so many small cafés, they also express our modernity in another way – they're predominantly a feature of our larger towns

and cities. Rapid urbanization of the industrial revolution left many living in squalid conditions and, crucially, without kitchens. This created a market for ready food, filled, for instance, with the invention of 'fish and chips' in Britain in the 1860s. Deep frying the potato transformed this staple food into something easily portable, while newly industrialized fishing methods made fish affordable and plentiful. As well as 'fish 'n' chips' take aways, relatively cheap fish restaurants sprung up that for the first time allowed the working classes to experience dining out. With waitress service and tables, these were precursors of our fast food restaurants, offering a very different experience from the inns that had provided informal food in previous times. Today, rising rents together with the pressures of space and time in large cities such as London, Tokyo and New York continue to drive innovations in casual eating.

The mechanization accompanying the industrial revolution led to increased mobility which created, in turn, new catering needs for travellers. These were initially met by elaborately fitted out dining cars on trains. In the USA, these gradually became stationary 'diners', retaining much of the aesthetics and format of the railway diner, but now catering

10

to the individual traveller in the automobile. These gave way to the 'drive in' in the 1950s, where consumers did not even have to get out of their cars, and then in the 1980s to the 'drive through', for the driver too restless to keep still.

Now fast food is changing again. As Dutch designer Frank Tjepkema points out, commenting on his design of sandwich bar Pluk in Haarlem, the Netherlands [p.176], we are now in 'a very interesting transition period, because in the eco and slow food age, fast food has to totally reinvent itself.' Just as radical social changes required innovative design before, so now is design pressed into action to develop fast food formats, interiors and graphics that respond to the new imperatives of sustainability.

And that includes McDonald's, which has embarked on a radical redesign program starting in its European restaurants [p.150]. Dropping its famous standardized, single overarching design philosophy, it now has a variety of interior styles, each introducing different elements more associated with up-market coffee houses and restaurants. Some designers, such as New York-based designer Ali Tayar (who designed the influential modern fast food restaurants Burger Bar and Pizza Bar [p.78], are nostalgic for the past

and the relinquishing of traditional bespoke elements in favour of 'high design'. Others, however, are fans, including Ab Rogers, who has redesigned the British roadside chain Little Chef [p.162]. 'It's very clever, brave and has interesting use of colour' he says. 'With Little Chef we were challenging the food product as well – we would have found it much harder to work on if that hadn't been the case.'

The classic eras of fast food saw a significant investment in design, something that isn't always the case today. 'It is hard to get fast food companies to get their head around investing in design,' says Ab Rogers, pointing out that the budget per square metre for the Little Chef project was less than half of what he would normally expect for a commercial interior.

While Little Chef called on the services a famous Michelin-starred chef, there are other ways in which the food itself can be reconsidered. Food design – practised by people like Mart Bretillot – features dishes designed (rather than 'cooked') to create shapes and experiences. Catalan designer Martí Guixé has also approached food as a material in pure design terms (he is unable to cook) as part of numerous projects and books, but also to evolve novel fast food concept, the Camper

11 Nestling in the Alps is the so called 'Eagle's Nest' or Kehlsteinhaus in the southern German town of Berchtesgaden, once the holiday retreat of Adolf Hitler and now repurposed as a destination coffee house.

12 Hafod Eryri, a remote visitor centre and café designed by Ray Hole Architects, located at the top of Snowdon, the highest point in Wales.

11

13 The original, discreet bamboo and
wood interior designed by Kengo
Kuma for Sake No Hana, a high
end Japanese sushi restaurant
opened in London by Alan Yau
in 2007.

14 A typical soda fountain pictured
in a diner in St Paul, Minnesota
in 1952.

FoodBALL restaurant in Barcelona [p.172]. Revered Japanese architect Kengo Kuma has gone so far as to suggest that architecture should learn from sushi. At an event in London in 2008 he said:

> 'Sushi is a good metaphor for my architecture. The importance in sushi is to choose the best material from the place, in season. If the journey of the ingredients is too long, the taste of the sushi is compromised. That is a problem that can't be solved by modern technology, and that program of using local material in season is the secret of good taste, and the secret of my style.'

Interesting as his comments are, they are nicely contradicted by his designs. Bamboo is not indigenous to London yet features in two stunning London restaurants he designed in 2008, one of which is the informal noodle bar Cha Cha Moon [p.108]. It would seem that Kuma too was unable to escape the 'theming' that characterizes fast food.

Small cafés and restaurants opening today do so in the shadow of a significant heritage that underwrites the food

and experience offered, and it is unusual for the designers not to reference these traditions. Snog in London [p.136], is a rare example that takes its cue instead from contemporary retail, and TangySweet [p.130] in Washington, DC, from nightclubs. Both, however, are part of the nascent frozen yogurt category that has yet to establish its own heritage.

No doubt other new concepts will follow. Many of these enjoy a surge of popularity before quickly dying out, such as the 19th and early 20th century American obsession with the sofa fountain. Its rise and fall is documented in John Jakle and Keith Sculle's fascinating study, *Fast Food: Roadside Restaurants in the Automobile Age*. While now associated with health problems, these dispensed carbonated drinks (including one that was to become the most famous of all brands – Coca-Cola) that were presented as having health-boosting properties and had originally been sold in pharmacies. As the craze for these carbonated drinks developed, cafeterias and 'luncheonettes' began to install elaborately designed, bar-sized dispensers in which the soda would be prepared and sold. A journalist writing in the 1920s in *The Soda Fountain*, a specialist trade magazine describes one of these as 'equipped with fine fixtures and decorated

15

with dignity and taste'. Today all that remains of these once extravagantly designed features is the small perfunctorily designed dispenser of the fast food chain, where a disposable beaker is pressed against a lever.

Other unlikely confection is ice cream. Initially an iced combination of fruit and wine, it gradually morphed into global ubiquity as ice cream, helped in no small part by the design and rituals of the ice cream parlour. Other informal eating concepts have established themselves even more rapidly. Take the packaged sandwich 'to go', pioneered by British retailer Marks & Spencer in the 1980s. It's now, only a few decades later, commonplace around the world, and is the staple of chains such as Pret A Manger, founded in 1986 in London but slowly expanding internationally. It sells pre-packaged sandwiches to either take away or eat on the premises in a café themed seating area, in a way that is quite distinct from the ways in which sandwiches had been sold previously by delicatessens, food stores and bakeries.

At its best, the design of a small café or fast food restaurant is a total design, taking in all the visual, social and service aspects required rather than merely a pretty interior. Conceptual 'eating designer' Marije Vogelzang who ran her own café [p.208] criticizes the limited interior design approach. 'I think it is a shame that interior designers stop short of thinking about the software of a place, which is really important,' she says. 'By software I mean, the details, the routing; it's about logistics and the people that work there, and what they wear. I think that's where there is a big gap between the designers of a place and the people who run it. A lot of designers just want to make a nice place to which they can put their name and says "hey, look what I have done".'

The forty projects from around the world that follow are a mixture of the practical and joyfully self indulgent. They are loosely grouped by category, and they all serve a common purpose, to provide food that can be eaten informally in a comfortable and pleasing environment.

15  Bangalore Express, an Indian
    restaurant in London designed
    by Outline, featuring booths
    and tables that are reached
    by ladders.

16  A customer eating and a chef in a
    diner in Dar es Salaam, Tanzania.

16

CAFÉS AND DELICATESSENS

**EAST BEACH CAFÉ**

Designers
THOMAS HEATHERWICK
STUDIO
Size
200 sq m (2153 sq ft)
total floor area including
kiosk
Date
2007
Location
LITTLEHAMPTON, UK

**CAFÉS AND
DELICATESSENS**

1 The oxidized shell of the East
  Beach Café is intended as a
  mysterious presence on the beach.

**EXPOSED TO WEATHER AND** vandalism, and, according
to Thomas Heatherwick, looking like a cross between the
rusting hull of a ship and a giant piece of driftwood, the East
Beach Café occupies pride of place on Littlehampton's sea
front. It's a building that manages to be visually exciting from
just about any angle and one that its designer suggested be
seen almost as something mysterious that had been washed
up on the beach.

Since the incredible reception that greeted Frank Gehry's
Guggenheim Museum, talk of the Bilbao effect has become
something of a cliché. And the building's overwhelming
success has inspired projects all over the world, in the hope
that commissioning a spectacular and iconic building could,
like magic, put as forlorn a place as the Northern Spanish
industrial city of Bilbao on the map.

Few, however, have come even close to recreating the
excitement and hype that greeted Gehry's shiny museum,
and its splashy, look-at-me approach to design may have
finally have fallen out of fashion. Yet one or two projects may
claim to be legitimate heirs.

One such is the East Beach Café in Littlehampton. One
of many forgotten, neglected and run-down British seaside

2 Section showing the steel casing and polyurethane foam interior insulation, finished with plaster together with concealed shuttering for the cafés glass front.

3 Floor plan showing layout of eating area; kitchen and kiosk are situated at one end of the building.

4 The café's structure appears as though made of interlocking metal ribbons.

resorts, Littlehampton is on the south coast of England, not far from Brighton. But Thomas Heatherwick's café design suddenly had people in the UK and abroad seeking Littlehampton out. Even before it was finished, the East Beach Café was a project that had people talking, partly due to the controversial nature of Thomas Heatherwick's work.

Planning considerations dictated the unusually narrow shape of the building, but the studio didn't want to end up with a structure dominated by 'flat, two-dimensional façades'. Instead, they describe it as 'sliced diagonally into ribbons that wrap up and over the building, forming a layered protective shell, open to the sea in front'. Each of these ribbons is 30 cm (12 in) wide and conceals retractable shutters to protect the glass windows and doors at night. The ribbons are made of steel, which is coated with a special oil treatment that allows for oxidization without compromising its structural integrity. The steel sections were fabricated locally and delivered in installments.

While the extraordinary exterior is the main attraction, the wavy interior space is also unusual. The effect is achieved using polyurethane foam that has been plastered. The result is a cave-like space that looks out to sea.

The project was conceived privately by mother and daughter Sophie Murray and Jane Wood to protect the seafront from plans for a much larger restaurant which they felt would lead to over-development. During the day the space operates as a café and kiosk, morphing into a more formal restaurant in the evening.

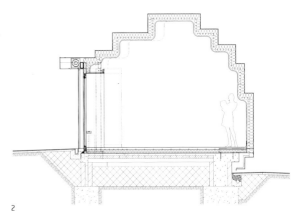

2

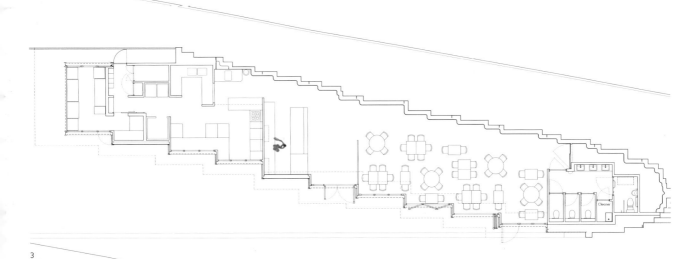

3

5

'DIAGONALLY SLICED INTO RIBBONS
THAT WRAP UP AND OVER THE BUILDING,
FORMING A LAYERED PROTECTIVE SHELL.'

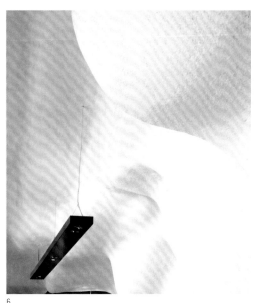

6

5 View over the adjoining car park to the back of the structure.

6 The softly undulating white surfaces of the interior are the result of plastering over polyurethane foam.

7 The café has a cave-like feel with a window only on one side of the long space, which looks out to sea.

8 Simple, classical furniture was specified by the client so as not to distract from the interior's design.

7

8

## THE ROYAL CAFÉ

Designers
**LO ØSTERGAARD AND RUD CHRISTIANSEN**
Size
**120 sq m (1292 sq ft)**
Date
**2007**
Location
**COPENHAGEN, DENMARK**

1 The whimsical interior seeks to present a 'funky Baroque' alternative to Scandinavian minimalism, while remaining characteristically Danish.

2 The main bar area of the café, showing how small design items are sold alongside cake and coffee.

2

**THERE IS LITTLE THAT** evokes Danish heritage more than the blue and white porcelain products of Royal Copenhagen. One of the oldest buildings in the Danish capital, dating back to 1616, serves as the porcelain manufacturer's home. Situated on one of the most important thoroughfares, the red brick building now also functions as Royal Copenhagen's flagship store and museum after an extensive refurbishment by Dorte Mandrup Arkitekter.

To the rear of the building, facing onto a courtyard, the Royal Café was opened by partners Lo Østergaard and Rud Christiansen. They already had experience of creating small eateries, with their diminutive and eccentric Kafferiet, which presents itself as the 'smallest café in the world'. Clearly, heritage had to be the order of the day for the Royal Café, and while the café was an unusually extensive example of product placement (you can choose which of Royal Copenhagen's dinner sets you want your food served on), it also had to have its own identity.

They successfully achieved this with an innovative food concept and the whimsical décor. The idea behind both was to take something central to Danish culture and, while treating it with respect, also give it a distinctive modern reinterpretation. For the food this meant the development of 'smushi'. Smørrebrød is a traditional Danish food – a simple sandwich that is adorned with a variety of toppings. But these sandwiches are also quite large. By combining the concept with sushi, the owners arrived at the word 'smushi'. While the name may be slightly tongue-in-cheek, the food itself is serious – tiny, open-faced sandwiches delicately piled with various delicacies. These are the café's signature dish, but naturally the full range of coffees and cakes and other café food are available too.

The interior design adopts a similarly quirky relationship to the Danish past. Danish design now tends to be firmly associated with rigorous Modernism or even minimalism, but the owners wanted to find a route back to something different that was equally Danish. 'Funky Baroque – design confusion, humorous and chic' is how Christiansen sums it up, adding that 'the design is 100 percent by both of us and a bottle of red wine!'. Naturally, porcelain figurines abound, but are not necessarily displayed in the way that you would expect. The space is not a slick unified design, nor was it intended as such. Its owners were clear that they wanted it to serve as an antidote to the generic 'Starbucks experience'

3  A traditionally dressed doll
   hangs over visitors to the café,
   contributing to its humorous and
   surreal atmosphere.

4  The café's light-hearted logo
   features a frog topped by a
   ballerina.

3

THE ROYAL CAFE

4

generally on offer, not only in Denmark but practically anywhere else in the world.

Danishness is expressed by the quirky coming together of very different products by Danish manufacturers such as Georg Jensen, Fritz Hansen, Bang & Olufsen, Kvadrat, Carlsberg and Holmegaard. Icons of Danish style from different eras somehow manage to sit side by side, and many of the items are for sale. The idea was always that the space would function as much as a shop as a café, but one where you could also try things out first.

Østergaard and Christiansen made great effort to source appropriate products for the Royal Café, and if these weren't already in production they encouraged manufacturers to create items that met their needs. 'Fritz Hansen have, for example, produced the Ant chair designed by Arne Jacobsen in a new counter-height size for the first time. Holmegaard Glass have produced the chandeliers according to our design, using their own expertise in glass-making. Royal Copenhagen adapted several serving items to suit the café environment and proper presentation of our new cuisine.'

The concept was created with an eye for international expansion, with its creators hoping that 'the Royal Café will

function and perform as a 'mini' Danish embassy, as we have incorporated design, history and cuisine from Denmark'. A similarly quirky website, replete with a jazz soundtrack, does a good job of recreating the flavour of the café online.

5 Classic Scandinavian furniture is used as part of a florid, highly decorative interior design.

6 Overview of the main seating area, demonstrating the eclectic and characterful elements that make up the café's interior, including a special extended version of Arne Jakobsen's classic Ant Chair, manufactured by Fritz Hansen.

'THE SPACE WOULD FUNCTION AS MUCH AS A SHOP AS A CAFÉ, BUT ONE WHERE YOU COULD ALSO TRY THINGS OUT FIRST.'

5

**COSO CAFÉ**

Designers
**FRANCESCO MONCADA
AND MASSIMO TEPEDINO**
Interior design
**ORNELLA GASBARRO**
Size
**90 sq m (969 sq ft)**
Date
**2006**
Location
**PALERMO, ITALY**

**CAFÉS AND
DELICATESSENS**

1

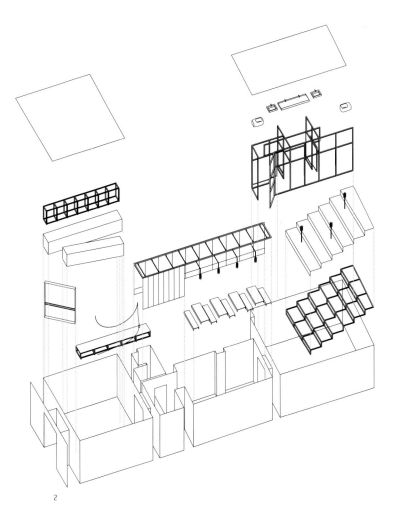

1 The use of bare industrial materials creates an unusually austere atmosphere for the interior of the Coso Café in Palermo.

2 Exploded diagram showing the interlocking elements of the three-room space.

3 Internal elevation showing the division of the café into three zones (with allusions to Sicily's infamous mafia).

2

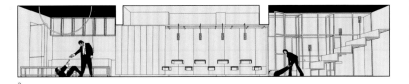

3

**THE ITALIAN NOTION OF** a café is a wide-ranging one, taking in anything from the traditional bar where people pop in for an espresso and a pastry, to a lounge bar offering alcoholic drinks. Coffee, it would seem, has become a generic basis for social interaction in a country addicted to the drink. It is these forms of social interaction that dominated the design process for Coso Café.

Located in a nineteenth-century building in the old town of the Sicilian capital Palermo, Coso is a café at the lounge end of the spectrum; one that makes little concession to the aesthetic conventions of hospitality. Clinically stark in terms of its aesthetics and materials, minimalist even, the design developed by Francesco Moncada, Massimo Tepedino and Ornella Gasbarro is, however, conceptually rich.

The designers created a seating system that allows union and intersection instead of exclusion. 'A stage, double-sided bench and a bench on wheels generates a shared space in which you can share the bench but not the table or you can be seated between strangers', they explain.

Throughout, industrial-looking materials are left bare to speak for themselves. One lighting feature is simply a circular fluorescent strip, while standard lightbulbs with

4

4 Plywood steps provide seating in
the final room, while the patterned
surfaces of sound insulation
panels on the walls provide a hint
of decoration.

5 View of glass front door and bar
area of the café.

exposed wiring light the rest of the space. The floor is simply
black-pigmented, polished concrete.

The café consists of three connected rooms leading back
into the space. The first is the bar area, which has drinks
stored on off-the-peg metal shelving normally used for tools
or books. Opposite it is an austere metal bench on castors.
You then go through an intermediate space, with storage
areas concealed behind Teflon panels, and a particularly
austere toilet arrangement. Steel benches and tables
emanate blankly from the wall to provide a social area.

The final room has a ramp of plywood on a steel support,
to create a kind of informal seating area similar to that
designed by Martí Guixé for Camper FoodBALL in Barcelona
(see page 172). Foam insulation panels are used on the
walls, their geometric surface adding a decorative element to
the design that is otherwise almost cruelly industrial.

As with Pizza Perez (see page 90), Moncada, Tepedino
and Gasbarro collaborated with each other and with
contractors by fax and email as all were living in different
countries, and only Gasbarro was in Sicily to oversee the
implementation of the project in the flesh.

## 'THROUGHOUT, INDUSTRIAL-LOOKING MATERIALS ARE LEFT BARE TO SPEAK FOR THEMSELVES.'

6

6 A simple steel trolley on castors
serves as customer seating in
the first zone of the café, opposite
the bar.

7

8

9

7 Cantilevered table and seating in the middle space of the café, with more exposed fluorescent lighting.

8&9 The toilet area has a clinical starkness, relieved by the introduction of a touch of colour.

ESPRESSO *K

Designers
**2012 ARCHITECTEN**
Size
**18 sq m (194 sq ft)**
Date
**2007**
Location
**DELFT, NETHERLANDS**

CAFÉS AND
DELICATESSENS

**LOOKING TRULY LIKE SOMETHING** that has landed from outer space, an alien structure sits in an atrium of the Delft University of Technology, where it serves as a popular espresso bar for the students of the Faculty of Architecture.

Despite appearing futuristic at first sight, the spaceship-like structure created by 2012 Architecten turns out to be an ingenious assemblage of industrial detritus. It is the fruition of various cycles of reuse. Not only have the materials from which it is constructed been reused, but so has this particular structure. It started out in 2003 as one of the Rotterdam-based practice's first serious forays into reusing waste as an architectural strategy.

Playing around with discarded white goods, they realized they could use washing machine fronts as modular elements for a larger structure. Five of these could be put together, carried by two people, and fitted through a standard door opening. These modules could then be bolted together and made watertight to create a caravan-like space. It transpired that the fronts of the washing machines of premium German manufacturer Miele proved easiest to use, which is why the project was initially christened the Miele Space Station. Despite its worthy eco-credentials, the structure maintains

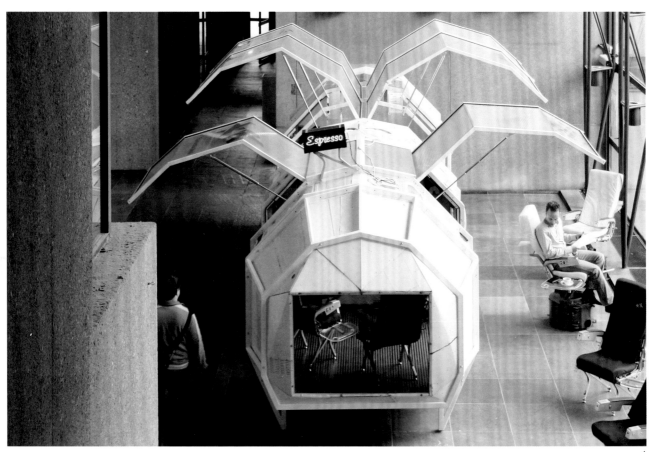

1

1 The café, situated in the foyer of the Delft University of Technology, like a spaceship that has just landed after an expedition to another planet.

2&3 The café-cum-spaceship was constructed in modular fashion from recycled Miele washing machines, whose doors now function as cabin-like windows and hatches.

2

3

4

4 A kitchen was added to the structure for its final use as a café, again using recycled materials, many of them scavenged for building works elsewhere on the campus.

5 A detail of one of the drawers showing the salvage of aircraft fittings, in this case the use of a seatbelt buckle as a drawer handle.

6 A montage of electronic circuit boards gave a futuristic feel to the internal seating area, which was furnished with chairs salvaged from a scrapped aircraft interior.

throughout a sense of humour derived from the disparity between its junk components and the high-tech futurism of an aircraft or spaceship.

The project then went through various stages of development, including the addition of a kitchen made from discarded fridge doors, before reaching its final resting place in response to the commission from the University of Delft, after Wytze Patijn, the Dean of the Faculty of Architecture, saw it at an exhibition and realized another use to which it could be put.

A bar and kitchen units were added to the structure, made from discarded billboards, while scrapped aircraft seatbelt clips serve as door handles. The doors were scavenged from materials discarded at building works taking place at a different part of the university building.

Scattered around the bar itself are a selection of airliner seats, which are now mounted on washing machine drums so that they can swivel. While these provide the main seating for those wishing to have their coffee on-site, there is also a 'microlounge' in the main structure. Hundreds of scrapped electronic circuitboards are used to create an atmospheric cladding for the tiny room, which the designers hoped would

have the air of a control room or cockpit. Two further modified aircraft seats are present, modified with a small tray on which to place your espresso.

In 2008 the university building was devastated by a fire on its upper stories. Even though the café structure was largely undamaged, its cycles of reuse finally came to an end and it was demolished along with the rest of the building.

5

'THE WASHING MACHINES OF GERMAN MANUFACTURER MIELE PROVED EASIEST TO USE.'

6

Designers
**DAVID COLLINS STUDIO**
Size
**60.5 sq m (651 sq ft)**
Date
**2009**
Location
**KILKENNY, IRELAND**

**JOHN STREET TEA AND WINE**

CAFÉS AND
DELICATESSENS

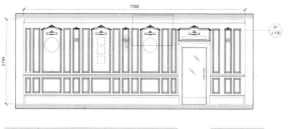

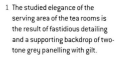

1 The studied elegance of the
    serving area of the tea rooms is
    the result of fastidious detailing
    and a supporting backdrop of two-
    tone grey panelling with gilt.

2 Floor plan and internal elevations
    showing the layout of the
    extensive panelling.

2

**ONE OF THE STAUNCHEST** advocates of traditional café and
restaurant interiors in recent years has been David Collins,
whose sensitive design and historical refurbishments of
a string of classic establishments have contributed to a
re-evaluation of the sumptuous, glamorous and luxurious
charms of various historical design idioms. Combining
modern design values with historically informed sensitivity
has allowed his studio's work to straddle the divide between
contemporary and traditional design, exemplified by these
tea rooms in the Irish city of Kilkenny.

Located on the river Nore about 100 km (62 miles)
south of Dublin, Kilkenny is a small city well-known for its
architectural heritage – most notably its medieval buildings,
but also some elegant Georgian buildings, one of which now
houses John Street Tea and Wine.

The client approached David Collins Studio with a brief
to design 'classically inspired tea rooms that would serve
handmade cakes, quality teas and fine wines'. The idea
behind the project was to create an alternative kind of
destination to the many typical pubs for which the city,
and indeed Ireland, is famous. The concept of the tea room
in Europe harks back to the eighteenth century fashion in
Britain and its colonies (which Ireland then was) to drink
tea and eat elegant snacks. Tea rooms became immensely
popular, growing in size, before largely disappearing after the
Second World War. The consumption of tea, however, in both
Ireland and Britain, remains a national obsession, but one
that is now largely conducted in private.

John Street Tea and Wine refers back to the traditional
Georgian tea parlour for inspiration, to create an 'intimate
room with the air of an exclusive private salon'.

The building that houses it was built around 1775 and
had seen a variety of uses, including serving as barracks
for the Royal Irish Constabulary for an extended period until
1925, when it was converted into two shops. While the basic
Georgian fabric was there, the designers needed to balance
their approach to the project between seeing it as sensitive
historical reconstruction (the building is listed), while also
creating a desirable and fashionable destination.

'We brought the concept of a traditional tea room into
the twenty-first century,' explains Simon Rawlings, creative
director at David Collins Studio. He took inspiration from
the original building, using this as the foundation of the
design. Two-tone grey lacquered panelling with gilt details

# 'WE TOOK INSPIRATION FROM THE ORIGINAL BUILDING AND USED THIS AS THE FOUNDATION OF THE DESIGN.'

3

4

is combined with a handcrafted Jacobean-style plaster ceiling. The 28 chairs were upholstered in royal blue leather, some with crocodile embossing, and the tables are topped with white marble. For the lighting, a mixture of antique and modern lighting was chosen, including a feature chandelier created by New York lighting designer David Weeks.

Rawlings sums up the approach, which might apply to the studio's work as a whole, as 'classic design elements with a twist, traditional references re-interpreted, and luxury reinvented.' As with so many of the studio's projects, the rooms look as though they have always been there, but without seeming like museum pieces.

One element that gives the room a subtle surreal tweak is the collection of porcelain, which forms part of the room's decoration. From a distance, blue and white glazed items seem totally traditional, the kind of antique china you might expect to find in any period room of the era. On closer inspection, however, they turn out to be quirky modern reinterpretations of classic Dutch porcelain. Part of the concept for the space is that it would feature a personal collection of contemporary porcelain by important designers and artists, which the owner intends to evolve by buying

pieces from around the world while travelling.

Shortly after opening, a courtyard area was opened to allow visitors to eat and drink outside.

3 Shelves of tea containers and glass pots function both as storage and decoration.

4&5 The owner's evolving collection of blue and white porcelain, both contemporary and antique, is an integral part of the design concept.

6 The designers sought to create
an 'intimate room with the air of a
private salon', using refined and
classic means with a slight hint
of modernity.

Designer
**STUDIO MYERSCOUGH**
Size
**40 sq m (431 sq ft)**
Date
**2008**
Location
**LONDON, UK**

1  The brightly painted train carriage
   that serves as a café is a surprising
   sight in the run down streets of the
   London suburb of Deptford.

'THEY JUST CAME UP with the idea of a train and said can you do something with this,' says London-based designer Morag Myerscough. 'We were allowed to do what we wanted and just had fun.'

So a 35-tonne 1960s railway carriage was laboriously transported to its resting place on Deptford High Street, one of London's more disadvantaged areas, by property developer Cathedral Group. This would house an unusual café that would signal the beginning of a large scheme to regenerate the area and bring some life and excitement to it. As well as being a café, The Deptford Project would also function as the space to host various community and artistic initiatives until the site, once a Victorian railway yard, is given over to the construction of major buildings by Richard Rogers and Alison Brooks Architects in 2011.

'Deptford is very colourful in some ways but not in others, such as architecture, so I wanted to make this colourful,' says Myerscough, who decided on a fun and vibrant graffiti-like scheme for the exterior of the train carriage. A raised platform was constructed out of recycled wood to run along the outside of the carriage, which was then furnished with plants sourced by the designer from Columbia Road Market

2 The exterior was painted using hand-cut stencils and features lyrics from a variety of train-themes songs.

so that it could function as a 'little outdoor oasis' for local residents. The platform also allows easy disabled entry into the train carriage through a large double door. This was cut into the steel exterior, and also served to increase the ventilation of the railway carriage; important, as it would house the kitchen as well as the main seating area.

Inside, a central table runs most of the length of the space that was constructed out of recycled school laboratory tables, which were then lacquered by a car spray technician. New legs were made by artist Luke Morgan, who was invited to collaborate on the project. The idea was that the table could be disassembled if required but, importantly, its centrally placed legs also allowed easy wheelchair access. The long table, says Myerscough, has been particularly effective allowing the space to become convivial and chatty as different people sit down next to each other; important given the community role intended for the café. Its design also meant up to 26 people could be accommodated inside the café-bistro.

The decoration along one side of the train relays the history of the area though images such as the rope (to denote Deptford's maritime heritage) while the other side features train-themed lyrics from songs. Some of these lyrics also appear on the tops of the stools inside, but these are related to the act of sitting. 'These are just lyrics that I like,' says Myerscough. 'After all, how often are you just given a train and allowed to do what you want to with it?' The painting of the train exterior was done by the designer and an assistant using hand-cut stencils.

They decided it would be better for the toilet to be housed outside the main carriage, so that was relegated to a garden shack. As Morgan 'was crazy about Elvis', Myerscough gave him free rein to create a toilet that could also be a shrine to The King. Visitors are encourage to take pictures of themselves in the gold mirror and send them on their mobile phones to become part of the decoration of the room.

The lampshades were sourced from the designer's own shop and are made from reused surgical tubing. The food follows the sustainable ethos of the design, using either locally or sustainably sourced ingredients.

2

3

3&4 A raised platform made of recycled wood serves as an outdoor seating area, serviced by a hatch cut into the train carriage.

5 The toilet was created by artist Luke Morgan as a shrine to Elvis.

'HOW OFTEN ARE YOU JUST GIVEN A TRAIN AND ALLOWED TO DO WHAT YOU WANT TO WITH IT?'

4

5

6 The seats, like the exterior, feature appropriate song lyrics.

7 Laboratory tables were recycled to create this long central table, intended to facilitate social interaction rather than individuals sat apart.

6   7

# REPÚBLICA CAFÉ

Designer
**ERNESTO DE CEANO AND
DCD INTERIORISMO**
Graphics
**SELEKO AND MOREAMORE**
Size
**122 sq m (1313 sq ft)**
Date
**2006**
Location
**SEVILLE, SPAIN**

**CAFÉS AND
DELICATESSENS**

**THE ALAMEDA DE HÉRCULES** is a characteristically sultry street in the southern city of Seville. Located in the historic centre, it's an avenue fringed with trees and palms which springs to life at night as bars and clubs catering to the city's youth open their doors. Only very recently was the street's traditional covering of white sand replaced with modern paving, but much of the historic character of the area remains.

In 2006, five friends from different walks of life collaborated to open the kind of café on Alameda de Hércules that they themselves would like to go to. The idea was for somewhere that would be open to all from noon to dawn and function as a springboard for various social and creative events, while becoming a club at night. The versatile kitchen would offer German cake and coffee in the afternoon, and beer and tapas later on.

Local designer Ernesto de Ceano was commissioned to design the space. He interpreted his clients' wish for a transparent and versatile space quite literally, creating a chameleon-like design that might at first sight appear bland but that could change from café or exhibition space to nightclub at the drop of a hat.

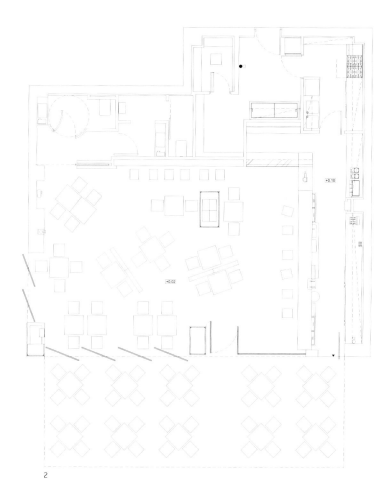

2

1  Simple white mobile plasterboard walls break up the space and support the strongly coloured lighting that allows the café to morph into a nightclub as the day progresses.

2. Floor plan showing an adaptable space that can spill out onto the pavement outside.

Floor-to-ceiling glass doors create a light and airy space, and can be opened to extend the space onto the terrace outside which, due to the Andalucian climate, can be used most of the year. Inside there are plasterboard walls that can be moved around to configure the space as required, creating small spaces for private events or book readings, or functioning as a screen on which films or presentations can be projected. For the second anniversary of its opening, the owners commissioned local graffiti artists Seleko and Moreamore to paint the walls, in keeping with their wish for the café to be a platform for like-minded people to have fun.

De Ceano compares his concept for the interior to a white tablecloth, something that could act as a background to something else. The materials used were simple, such as the polished concrete floor and plasterboard walls, and the room was simply painted white. When the walls aren't in use for an exhibition or special decoration such as the graffiti, he devised a flexible interior decoration scheme using coloured lighting to create different moods as required. Pre-programmed LED lighting bathes the space in different colours, in synch with the music played by DJs in the evening, again transforming the space.

# 'THE CONCEPT FOR THE INTERIOR WAS LIKE A WHITE TABLECLOTH, SOMETHING THAT COULD ACT AS A BACKGROUND TO SOMETHING ELSE.'

3

3 The simple bar area is dominated
 by two oversized ceiling-mounted
 lights that are programmed to
 change colour.

4 Detail of one of the curved flexible
 walls used to divide up the space.

4

5&6 The flexible wall panels allow for continually changing exhibitions, hosting artwork, projections or, as is the case here, graffiti painted by local artists Seleko and Moreamore.

5

6

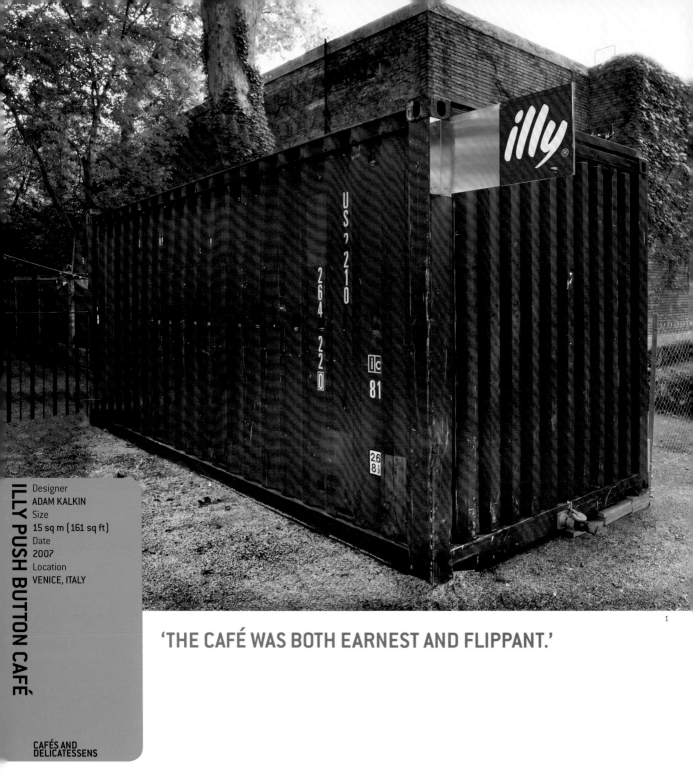

**ILLY PUSH BUTTON CAFÉ**

Designer
ADAM KALKIN
Size
15 sq m (161 sq ft)
Date
2007
Location
VENICE, ITALY

'THE CAFÉ WAS BOTH EARNEST AND FLIPPANT.'

1 Closed up at night, only the illy
sign gave the game away that the
rusted structure was anything
other than a plain shipping
container

2 Plan showing the layout of the
café's various functions when the
walls are opened and lowered.

**THE 17 MILLION OR** so shipping containers in use around the world have long intrigued designers looking for innovative and reusable readymade structures. Even if the expense of using them has been rather impractical, their rusting, corrugated exteriors have become markers for a readily identifiable 'container chic' and some undeniably ingenious design solutions.

One of the best known interrogators of the container form is eccentric American conceptual artist and architect Adam Kalkin and his practice, Architecture and Hygiene. His most famous structure, Bunny Lane, completely encloses an innocuous two-storey house in a readymade hangar structure, but he is also well known for his 'push button houses'. These are containers converted to hydraulically open at the push of a button, revealing all the utilities of a normal dwelling. The effect is somewhat surreal; a bit like an episode from a movie by Luis Buñuel.

Having been previewed at Art Basel Miami Beach, the push button house was brought over to Italy for the 2007 Venice Biennale. There it was reconfigured as a small espresso bar that its sponsors, Italian coffee brand illy, suggested 'opened like a flower'.

Part conceptual artwork, part photogenic, branded marketing ploy, the illy Push Button House also managed to meet its functional requirements. The standard 6-m (20-ft) container was kitted out with three espresso machines and served coffee to visitors to the Biennale. A small lounge area was available for those who wanted to sit down and drink their coffee more slowly. The materials used, like that of the container itself, were all recyclable. At night or when not in use, the container sides could be drawn back up, leaving only the little 'illy' sign to advertise its function.

Like many of Kalkin's other projects, the illy café was both earnest and flippant, inviting creative engagement with many of the assumed features of the buildings around us and providing an effective if not entirely serious alternative. However, through Quik House, the commercial venture established by Kalkin to enable others to easily create their own container residences, so the possibility exists — at least theoretically — to create other container cafés or restaurants.

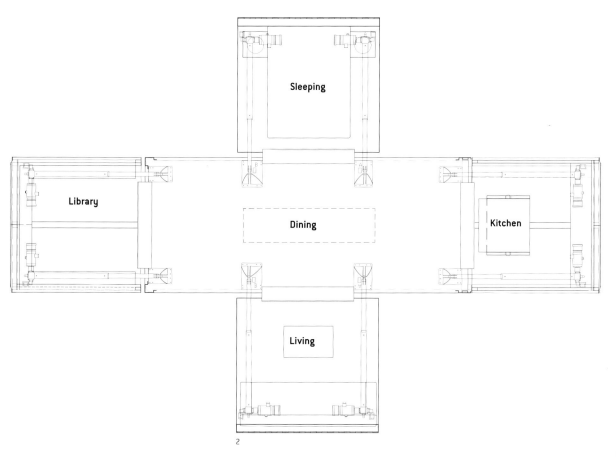

Sleeping

Library

Dining

Kitchen

Living

2

3

3 At the touch of a button, the
  walls of the container opened
  to reveal a fully appointed and
  functional café.

4&5 Long and short sections of the
  café in open mode.

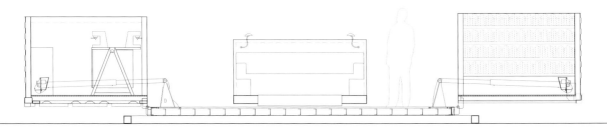

4

6

5 The open-plan toilet was probably
more about making a point than
offering an actual service that
visitors would use.

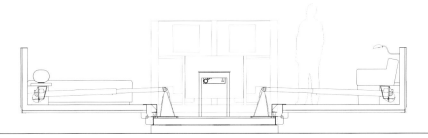

# THE PLANT CAFÉ ORGANIC

Designers
**CCS ARCHITECTURE**
Size
**185 sq m (1991 sq ft)**
Date
**2005**
Location
**SAN FRANCISCO, USA**

**CAFÉS AND
DELICATESSENS**

# 'MADE OF HICKORY, THE SLATS CREATE A WARM AND NATURAL ATMOSPHERE.'

2 Floor plan
1) Entry
2) Outdoor dining
3) Raised dining
4) Condiments and coffee
5) Storage
6) Point of sale
7) Juice Preparation
8) Salad Preparation
9) 'Grab'n'Go
10) Restroom
11) Main dining area
12) Condiments and water
13) Office
14) Kitchen

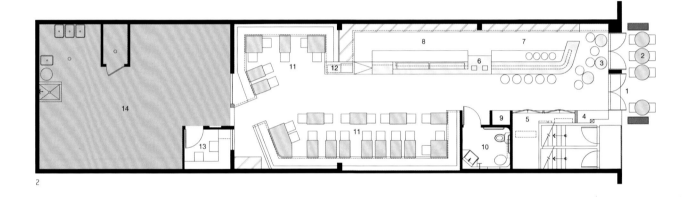

2

1 Delicate hickory slats create a warm, inviting and natural atmosphere for customers wanting to stay on the premises rather than take their food or drinks away.

**SAN FRANCISCO IS FAMED** for many things, including the penchant of many of its inhabitants for healthy eating. One of the many places you can get a healthy meal is at The Plant Café Organic, in the city's Marina district.

Owners Mark Lewis and Matthew Guelke wanted to open a café that would serve a variety of organic food and drink, and briefed CCS Architecture to design an interior that would be relaxed yet classy, but which also needed to express the values inherent in the organic health foods that were its raison d'être.

These values were interpreted as 'warmth, health and durability' by the designers, who relied heavily on their choice of materials for expression. Reclaimed and natural materials that are both long-lasting and durable, such as zinc, solid wood and stainless steel, allowed for the space to age and change, as well as reducing the amount of material to be used over time, say the architects.

The concept was for a counter-service restaurant and bar that would seat 50 people. Unsurprisingly the bar, made of hickory, glass, tile and brushed zinc, is a dominant feature of the café. The area behind the counter is given over to adjustable shelving, on which the produce is stored. As with

traditional delicatessens, this allows the changing foodstuffs and their packaging to be a principal decorative element.

The café could have been overwhelmed by this counter, so to lessen its impact and prevent it dominating the space, the project team hit upon the idea of creating a delicately slatted wall and ceiling over the seated dining area. It is this that becomes the café's most recognizable feature. Made of hickory, the slats create a warm and natural atmosphere supported by the suffused lighting. While the counter also serves for the office workers impatiently waiting for a takeaway lunch, it was important that the seated area was more welcoming, for those customers who wanted a more relaxing, slow meal.

Another environmental aspect of the design was to preserve as much natural light as possible – the kitchen was skylit while the glass doors to the front made for a welcoming entrance.

3

4

3 Detail of the patterns created by
the irregular hickory slats.

4 The long zinc covered bar
dominated the café, and is
divided into sections for salads
and for juices.

5

5 The hickory slats continue into
the roof to give a cosy feel to the
dining area.

6 Simple wood furniture and
shelving maintains the effect
created by the slatting, here
also seen reflected in the mirrors
along the seating area that
continues on from the bar.

# SILVER CAFÉ

Designers
**ARCA**
Size
**107 sq m (1152 sq ft)**
Date
**2008**
Location
**MORECAMBE, UK**

CAFÉS AND
DELICATESSENS

2

# 'IT IS LIKE A GIANT CINEMA SCREEN, WITH THE LIGHT CHANGING CONSTANTLY.'

**MORECAMBE IS A TYPICALLY** down-at-heel English seaside town. Formerly one of the major resorts in the North of England on account of its large bay, it has since developed a reputation as a dreary backwater. Keen to dispel this, the local authority commissioned Arca, a young practice located in nearby Manchester, to design a café that would seat between 40 and 50 people, envisioning a simple bunkered structure that would act as a focal point for locals and visitors to the area, as well as acting as a clear signal of Morecambe's regeneration.

'Having worked in Morecambe before, I knew that this was a very distinctive location,' says John Lee, principal of Arca. One of the first things that he did was change the brief to create a structure that, rather than hiding itself, would sit as high as possible to allow visitors to see over the barriers and across the bay and sea. A see-through pavilion-like structure was created, which is more complex than it first appears as it twists on its axis. It's almost like an extended walk-in periscope.

'From inside you get really great views; you can see the weather changing,' says Lee. 'It is like a giant cinema screen, with the light changing constantly. And from outside you can

3

see right through the building, which stops it from being an obstacle.'

Lee says he came to the project without any preconceptions, and at no point set out to create or engage with traditional seaside cafés or restaurants. The approach was sculptural, and the references were primarily taken from the work of sculptors like Richard Serra and Anish Kapoor.

The steel cladding was chosen to be robust enough to protect the building in such a tough marine environment, but Lee was also impressed by the way its sheen would work with the tones of the sky and sea, subtly engaging with the light rather than merely reflecting it.

The architects provided the envelope and lighting while the graphics and interior fit-out were carried out separately by the concession's tenant, Marc Holley. Holley had worked for a while as a troubleshooting consultant for restaurants before deciding to work for himself and winning the tender for this restaurant. The interior fit-out was simply carried out by him and his wife, with chairs and tables sourced from high street retailers and the graphics produced by local sign-makers.

Some people, Holley says, just sit with a cup of tea and spend hours gazing out over the endlessly changing panorama. But there are also plenty of local business people coming in for lunch, as well as visits from local politicians from all over the country eager to see the impact projects such as this can have on the local area. Holley tries to make sure that the food is as innovative as the building.

By law a single disabled toilet is included in the main structure, while a separate toilet block that also functions as a public amenity stands some way apart and has contrasting doors and fittings made of oak.

4

4 The stark geometry of the building also allows for a shading front overhang.

5 Floor plan
  1] Main seating area
  2] Kitchen/serving area
  3] Disabled toilet

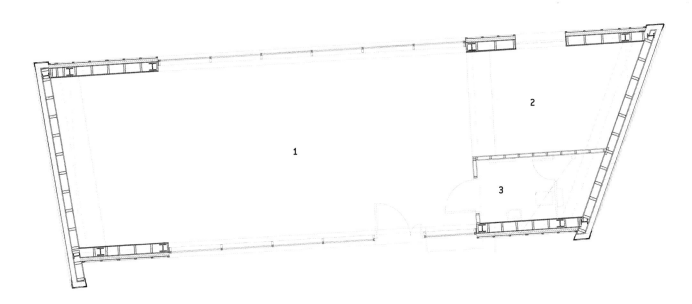

5

6 The glass front allows for the seascape to act as a giant mesmerizing screen for visitors to the café. The furniture was chosen by the café's tenants.

75

PIZZERIAS, PASTA RESTAURANTS AND TAPAS BARS

PIZZA BAR

Designers
ALI TAYAR, PARALLEL
DESIGN
Graphics
GIOVANNI RUSSO
Size
160 sq m (1222 sq ft)
Date
2008
Location
NEW YORK, USA

PIZZERIAS, PASTA
RESTAURANTS AND
TAPAS BARS

# 'DURING THE DAY, THE GEOMETRIC PATTERNS WERE WHITE, BUT AS NIGHT FELL THESE BEGAN TO GLOW A FLUORESCENT BLUE.'

1 DayGlo geometric patterns and a dramatically lit Corian bar created an exciting environment that alluded to classic Americana.

2 Allowing the colourful interior to create a theatrical effect for passers-by was an important consideration in the design.

**PIZZA BAR WAS AN** attempt to follow on from the runaway success of Pop Burger in New York's Meatpacking district. Also designed by Ali Tayar for clients Roy Liebenthal and Sasha Tcherevkoff, Pop Burger managed to give a fresh slant on fast food, serving it in a beautifully designed environment that, as the evening progresses, slowly morphs into a cocktail bar and stylish hangout. After Pop Burger, fast food joints opening in New York suddenly had to take their design very seriously.

Located a few doors down, Pizza Bar took the same idea and interpreted it to fit a smaller space. But this time, instead of hamburgers, pizza was the main item on the menu. The biggest design challenge was to create an environment that could fulfil its gradually changing role from pizza joint by day to lounge bar by night.

Tayar decided that the view from the street was paramount and conceived Pizza Bar almost as a theatrical set with a dazzling lighting scheme worthy of the stage. The exposed wooden ceiling beams were decorated with a pattern created by the artist Giovanni Russo. These were covered paper printed with DayGlo fluorescent paint — during the day, the geometric patterns on the wood were white, but as night

2

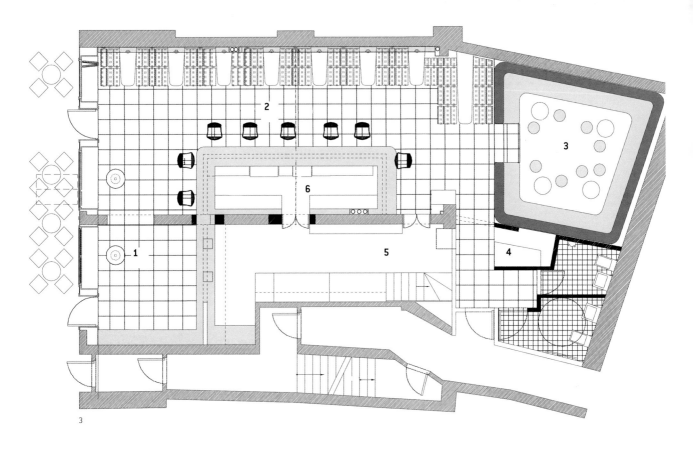

3

fell and the special black lights were turned on these began
to glow a fluorescent blue. The ceiling between the wooden
beams, visible only from inside the restaurant, featured the
pattern in an even more colourful extension. Silver Mylar
wallpaper was printed in six DayGlo colours to create this
luminescent, geometric design.

The vibrant colours engaged with the pop culture of the
1950s through to the 1980s that were very much part of
the concept of both the Pizza Bar and its hamburger-serving
siblings. The exposed brick wall was very New York, and the
other elements harked back in different ways to the neon
and plastic glory days of Americana, from the glitz of the
1980s to the diners and drive-ins of the 1950s.

'We would go to Coney Island and look around,' says
Tayar. 'But the main source of inspiration was the kind of
pizza joint you used to find on university campuses and
the psychedelic ballroom of the Palladium, a 1980s' club
of a time when high art was still involved in clubs and pop
culture.' Fiorucci, the fashion brand famed in the 1980s for
its low-cost, colourful high fashion, was another reference,
says Tayar.

The Corian bar (also treated to glamorous night-time
lighting) and the mixture of custom-made furniture and
iconic classics managed to avoid creating an effect of kitsch
retro. The booths had curious seats upholstered in blue vinyl.
Tayar says that these were inspired by the cushions on
modern gym machines, but they also managed to evoke the
nostalgia years of American fast food.

At the rear of the space was an area that became more
important as day progressed into night, and the emphasis
changed from pizza to bar. Design-wise, everything was
kept low in height if not impact, with a curved banquette and
stools, this time upholstered in synthetic red and fake blue-
dyed fur. Small tables also took turns as ice buckets.

But in the end Pizza Bar proved too big a stretch, and
its small, rather expensive, pizzas didn't have quite the pull
of the healthy burgers of its big brother Pop Burger next
door. While Pizza Bar looked stunning, it also only served to
cannibalize Pop Burger's custom without generating enough
of its own, and was soon closed down.

3 Floor plan
   1) Cafeteria
   2) Restaurant
   3) Lounge
   4) DJ booth
   5) Kitchen
   6) Bar

4 The blue vinyl seating of the main eating area was inspired by modern gym machinery but also evokes the design of classical American diners.

4

5

6

5 Artist Giovanni Russo created a pop art design for the exposed ceiling beams that would shine in DayGlo blue as night fell, with an even more colourful design on the ceiling that could be seen once you entered Pizza Bar.

6 View over the Corian bar, with classic wire bar stools designed by Harry Bertoia, to the street outside.

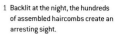

**YOU GET THE FEELING** that if Spanish film-maker Pedro Almodóvar were to design a tapas bar, it would look something like this. Estado Puro has an enviable location, situated right next to two of Madrid's prime attractions – the Prado Museum and the fountains of the Plaza de Neptuno. Located in the ground floor of a hotel, the NH Paseo del Prado, Estado Puro is, however, largely self-sufficient and has a distinctive, extrovert identity all of its own.

'Tapas 2.0' is how the bar describes its fare. The kitchen was in the charge of renowned Madrileño chef Paco Roncero, gastronomic director of the NH Group and also chef of the extravagant Jaime Hayon-designed La Terraza del Casino de Madrid. Roncero wanted to bring a fresh perspective to tapas, the quintessentially Spanish bar food that was perhaps suffering from over-exposure internationally. While classics such as gazpacho and tortilla are indeed on the menu, other more unexpected dishes are also offered, varying from delicacies such as foie gras with lentils to the slightly out-of-place hamburgers.

James & Mau, a practice led by Jaime Gaztelu and Mauricio Galeano, with offices in Chile, Spain and Columbia, was brought on board to design the new tapas bar. They

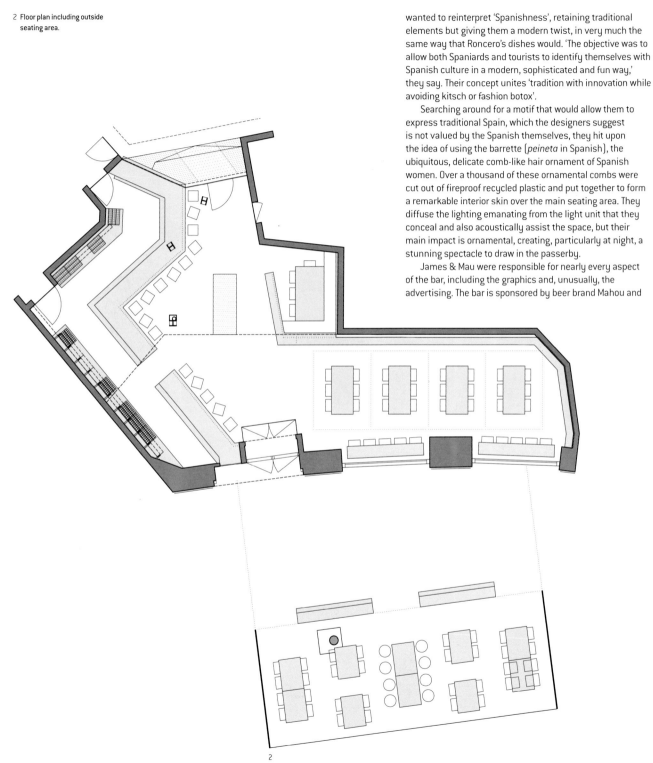

wanted to reinterpret 'Spanishness', retaining traditional elements but giving them a modern twist, in very much the same way that Roncero's dishes would. 'The objective was to allow both Spaniards and tourists to identify themselves with Spanish culture in a modern, sophisticated and fun way,' they say. Their concept unites 'tradition with innovation while avoiding kitsch or fashion botox'.

Searching around for a motif that would allow them to express traditional Spain, which the designers suggest is not valued by the Spanish themselves, they hit upon the idea of using the barrette (*peineta* in Spanish), the ubiquitous, delicate comb-like hair ornament of Spanish women. Over a thousand of these ornamental combs were cut out of fireproof recycled plastic and put together to form a remarkable interior skin over the main seating area. They diffuse the lighting emanating from the light unit that they conceal and also acoustically assist the space, but their main impact is ornamental, creating, particularly at night, a stunning spectacle to draw in the passerby.

James & Mau were responsible for nearly every aspect of the bar, including the graphics and, unusually, the advertising. The bar is sponsored by beer brand Mahou and

2

3

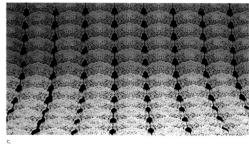

5

4

# 'OVER A THOUSAND ORNAMENTAL COMBS WERE PUT TOGETHER TO FORM A REMARKABLE INTERIOR SKIN.'

its advertising had to somehow be incorporated into the design. Making a virtue of necessity, James & Mau dug out an image from a 1961 advertising campaign and digitally manipulated the image to add the barrette, which has become the emblem of the restaurant, to the model's hair. Painted on the right-hand wall it livens up the space while continuing to play with the idea of 'Spanishness'. Likewise, the red stools and chairs outside are intended to evoke the red rose traditionally worn in the hair by Spanish women.

Spatially, it was important to orient the restaurant outwards, to integrate the external terrace and do justice to the fountain of Neptune spouting water in the square outside. James & Mau's solution was to curve the intricate wall and ceiling in such a way as to almost project attention through the window. Another of the architects' aims was to was break with conventions as to where the bar itself should be situated. Unusually, it zig-zags along the left wall and is made up of an enormous piece of white marble from Macael, in the south of Spain. Traditionally, Spanish bar counters are made of light-coloured marble, but of a thin and polished slab rather than the roughly hewn lump used here. This raw marble is a reference to the tapas bar's name,

which translates as 'pure state', as is the tiny glass-framed garden in the middle of the space. Outside there is another, larger, garden that is part of the terrace, and includes an area around a tree planted with vegetables used in the preparation of the tapas.

To create a feature for the door and the transitional space between the bar and the hotel, James & Mau collaborated with a group called NI. This feature was also inspired by traditional Spanish jewellery, with black bangles dangling from string.

6 A 1961 advertising image by Spanish beer brand Mahou was digitally reworked to provide a lively illustration for the end wall, while the assembled barrette appear as backlit lace.

1 View of the main seating area showing the simple use of industrial materials and the central divider that also serves as storage area.

2 The pizzeria is located on the ground floor of a plain 1970s office building, and its large glass frontage is opened in the Summer.

2

# 'COLOURED DOTS ARE PAINTED ON THE WALLS AND LINK UP IN A SEEMINGLY SCIENTIFIC MATRIX.'

**THE ANCIENT CITY OF** Siracusa (or Syracuse), located at the southern tip of Sicily, was an important place in Classical times, before slowly becoming a slightly forgotten and impoverished backwater. However, tourists who do seek it out are rewarded with a number of interesting sights, including a World Heritage Site that includes a cave known as the Tomb of Archimedes, in which it is claimed the famous Greek mathematician is buried. Close to this ruin cut from rock is a building of a very different in nature.

Located on the ground floor of a typical 1970s structure, in what is now the bustling business district of the city, is a colourful and distinctive pizzeria. Pizza Perez was designed on a shoestring by Francesco Moncada, who had returned to his hometown of Syracuse after stints with Foreign Office Architects in London and the Office for Metropolitan Architecture, Rotterdam. The restaurant takes its name from its owner – Vicenzo Perez – and aims simply to be a fun and lively venue.

Because of the budget constraints, it was decided that the primary decoration should be graphic. Point Supreme, a consultancy based in Athens, devised a vibrant scheme in which the various ingredients would be represented

1

3 Floor plan
  1) Fast food room
  2) Storage area
  3) 'Slow food' room
  4) Kitchen for the pizzeria
  5) Kitchen for the restaurant
  6) Toilets

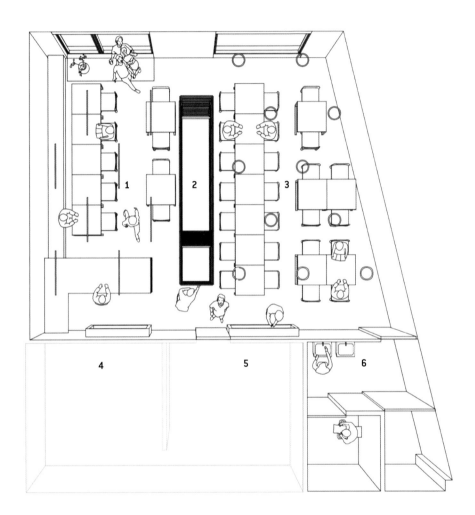

3

schematically by a coloured dot. These coloured dots are painted on the walls and link up in a seemingly scientific matrix to suggest the different toppings you can have on your pizza. The pizzeria's menu groups various pizzas according to time of year, and dots are used to colour-code the seasons (white/blue for Winter, green for Spring, red for summer and ochre for Autumn).

The antidote to all this colour is a larger-than-life zebra painted on the opposite wall, its black and white stripes providing a nice contrast to the coloured dots. 'It simply stands there: beautiful, mysterious, surreal and inspiring endless thoughts and discussions among the customers waiting for a table or some takeaway food,' says Moncada. It is also large enough to be seen through the glass front and pique the curiosity of people walking by.

Moncada split the restaurant into two areas, which are divided by a central fibreglass wall. This wall is transparent and used for everything from storing pizza ingredients to functioning as a place where customers can leave their coats and bags. One side of the central wall is a more social seating area for customers having their pizzas on-site, while the other, on the side that you enter, is intended for those

fetching a takeaway and wanting to drink a beer while they are waiting.

Making a virtue out of commercial necessity, the tables were placed right next to one another in such a way as to facilitate interaction. Similarly, no attempt was made to disguise the simple, cheap materials used in the restaurant's fit-out. The rear wall and floor are constructed from bare plywood, while translucent corrugated fibreglass panels are used for the ceiling, behind which off-the-shelf industrial lighting units are fitted. The toilets were simply given a lick of waterproof paint. In the summer, the glass front opens up and the restaurant spills onto the pavement outside.

4

5

4 The over-sized zebra conceived by Point Supreme livens up the space.

5 View through hatch in the central wall to the 'slow food' section.

6

6 The colour matrix of pizza ingredients devised by Point Supreme for the wall of the 'slow food' eating area.

7&8 Only the simplest, inexpensive materials were used, such as bare plywood, corrugated fibreglass and standard industrial fluorescent lighting fixtures.

9 The walls of the toilets are painted vivid orange to contrast with the white and translucent materials of the main restaurant areas.

7

8

9

LA CASA AZUL

Designers:
HERME LISCAR AND
MÓNICA GARCÍA
Size
19 sq m (205 sq ft)
Date
2002
Location
VALENCIA, SPAIN

PIZZERIAS, PASTA
RESTAURANTS AND
TAPAS BARS

1

# 'WE WERE INSPIRED BY THE IMAGE OF A LAZY SUNDAY SPENT IN THE SHADOW OF A VINE, HAVING A SIESTA WITH A GOOD BOOK.'

2

1 The historical building in the heart of Valencia's old town was restored to its original blue, from which the vinoteca and hotel take their name.

2 The vinoteca is dominated by the intricate shelves which seem to grow and extend like vines over the tight space.

**IN THE HISTORIC CENTRE** of the Spanish city of Valencia, a stone's throw from La Lonja de la Seda, the famous late-Gothic silk exchange, is a tiny *vinoteca* and hotel. A quirky yet respectful presence, La Casa Azul is the labour of love of Vicente Grace, a jeweller who decided to try his hand at winemaking.

Having worked with young design duo Herme Ciscar and Mónica García previously on an exhibition of his jewellery, Grace turned to them to design the small wine bar, or *vinoteca*. The idea was for a place where he could serve and sell wine from his own vineyard and incorporate a tiny three-room hotel and terrace above. The nineteenth-century building that would house the venture had been known as the 'house of cod', but its renovation showed that it had originally been painted blue, and this discovery gave the structure its new name.

For the *vinoteca*, the designers chose not to make a space that would come across as overtly commercial. Instead they went for a more domestic feel, creating an environment that uses traditional local design cues, but with a modern twist. 'Our intention was to create a cosy, warm, and above all, familiar space,' they say. 'We were inspired by

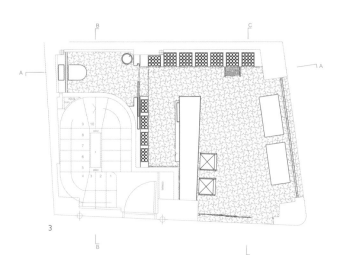

3

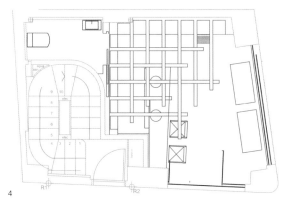

4

3 Plan showing the layout of the
rooftop terrace.

4 Floor plan of the diminutive
vinoteca, showing the trellis-like
carpentry.

the image of a lazy Sunday spent in the shadow of a vine, having a siesta with a good book.'

The wine (and also expensive Italian coffee-table books) is presented on wooden shelving which seems to grow into the space, starting as a trellis and then assuming shapes like vines. Like giant hams, two Campenela lamps, designed previously by Herme Ciscar and Mónica García, hang above the counter. 'Although we had made them two years before, they seemed designed for this place,' they say. The lamps suggest another reference – the protective paper bags that prevent ripening grapes succumbing to insects.

At first sight the tiled floor seems completely traditional, but on closer inspection it continues the thematic approach. The specially created ceramic tiles, both in the bar and in the toilets, are designed to mimic the effect of the vine leaves that have fallen to the ground. These were drawn by a friend from Cadiz, Adolfo Gonzalez Correa, and fired by local specialists La Cerámica Valenciana.

The bar itself, on which the food is served, is conceived to be like a side table in a domestic dining room; all appliances are hidden from sight. Two smaller tables are painted in light blue.

Each of the three bedrooms above has a different, locally-inspired theme, while at the top of the house is a terrace to which guests of the *vinoteca* or hotel can retreat. It too manages to combine traditional Spanish elements with modern whimsy.

5 The toilet showing geometric tiles suggestive of fallen vine leaves were designed by Adolfo Gonzalez Correa and fired by local specialists.

6 The terrace, available to guests of both the vinoteca and hotel, combines traditional Spanish elements with a modern twist. Valencia's famous La Lonja de la Seda, the medieval silk exchange, is visible from the terrace at the top of the building.

AS WITH SO MANY other nations, the Dutch love Italian food, yet the 'pasta to go' concept was still a novelty. However Servex BV, a subsidiary of the national rail service, decided to develop the idea and introduce it as a fast food option at railway stations in the Netherlands. The idea was for a meal that could be prepared in 90 seconds, allowing customers to choose the kind of pasta and type of sauce they wanted.

Integral to the concept was an interior with conspicuously higher design values than usual fast food restaurants at a railway station. Competing head to head with restaurants such as the multinational hamburger franchises, Servex felt that design could be an important differentiator and underpin the brand values through people's perceptions of Italy and beauty.

Amsterdam-based architects Merkx+Girod were appointed to develop the interiors, and the well-known graphic designer Irma Boon (better known for her book designs) and illustrator Agata Zwierzynska were also brought on board. Together they developed a narrative that would determine all aspects of the branding and design of the restaurant, at the heart of which lay 'Julia, a typical strong Italian woman, offering you a glimpse of her kitchen'.

1 View over the angled central table, showing the conspicuous use of high quality materials such as Corian and leather not usually associated with railway station fast food outlets.

2 Floor plan
  1 ] Entrance
  2 ] Teller and coffee counter
  3 ] Fresh pasta counter
  4 ] Work bench
  5 ] Coffee bar
  6 ] Reading table
  7 ] Seating area
  8 ] Toilets
  9 ] Kitchen
  10 ] Storage

2

103

3 View from the main station thoroughfare into Julia's, intended to appeal to travellers on account of its clean lines and evident design values.

The resulting design features an open kitchen intended to create a welcoming and transparent environment. Unusually expensive materials were specified, which had the added benefit of being able to resist the abuse and heavy wear experienced by a restaurant such as this.

Three angled Corian counters serve pasta, the sauce and the coffee in sequence, with kitchen paraphernalia left visible to create a quality feel and an air of domestic informality. Seating is at wooden benches or leather-upholstered chairs, which are either at the central canteen table made of Corian or at smaller, individual wooden tables. For those wishing to take food away, the pasta is placed in cardboard containers of the kind more often used for Chinese takeaways.

'Clean, healthy, pure, honest and natural' were the key words that guided the designers in their task. While the design has been criticized by some as being 'clinical', it does, however, project hygiene as a value; something that can be an important consideration for many potential customers when choosing between different fast food options.

Another benefit of the unusually expensive-looking interior and specification of quality materials, say the designers, is that the restaurant is treated with greater respect by diners, who tend to clear up after themselves and leave less rubbish than usual for a fast food joint.

Decoration of the space is minimal, with the actual materials themselves allowed to create the atmosphere. However the green apostrophe present in the sans-serif logo designed by Irma Boon (suggestive of a fashion boutique rather than a restaurant) is picked up in the green rubbish bins. Discreet drawings of pasta by Agata Zwierzynska adorn the walls.

The first restaurant was opened in Amsterdam's Central Station in 2008, and was quickly followed by another in Leiden, ahead of a roll-out across the Netherlands.

4

'DINERS TEND TO CLEAR UP AFTER THEMSELVES AND LEAVE LESS RUBBISH.'

4 Leather upholstered chairs surround the central Corian canteen table, while wooden benches and upholstered stools are supplied for the individual wooden tables at the perimeter of the restaurant.

SUSHI AND NOODLE BARS

**CHA CHA MOON**

Designers
**KENGO KUMA & ASSOCIATES (interior), NORTH DESIGN LONDON AND GRAPH DESIGN, TOKYO**
Size
**200 sq m (2153 sq ft) public areas**
Date
**2009**
Location
**LONDON, UK**

SUSHI AND NOODLE BARS

1 View along the rear wall where
mirrors make the converging lines
of the suspended bamboo poles
extend yet further.

2 Floor plan
1) Dining space
2) Bar
3) Male toilet
4) Female toilet
5) Disabled toilet
6) Storage
7) Office
8) Kitchen

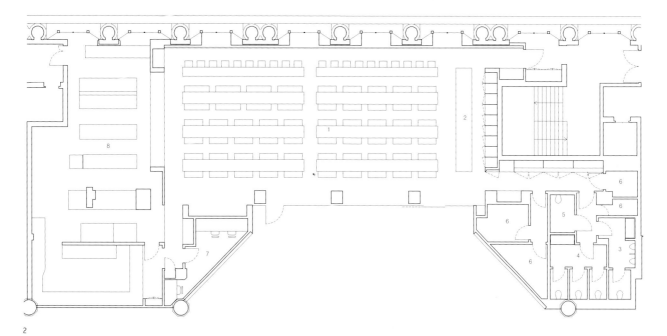

2

# 'EVERY FEW MINUTES, HIDDEN HUMIDIFIERS GENTLY SQUIRT A MIST OF WATER ONTO THE BAMBOO POLES.'

**IF THERE IS ONE** person who can be most credited with improving the aesthetic experience of London's diners it is Hong Kong-born restaurateur Alan Yau. Jaded palettes have been wowed by a succession of restaurants of the very highest design quality, such as atmospherically dark, very luxurious (and expensive) dim sum restaurant Hakkasan, designed by French interior designer Christian Liaigre. His first venture, Wagamama, which first opened its doors in 1992, has now been spun off into a highly successful global company and the many innovations introduced by the canteen concept have been widely emulated. The first Wagamama restaurant was a collaboration with minimalist architect John Pawson, and paved the way for a succession of projects that demonstrated Yau's ability to put design centre-stage and an unusual willingness to seek out and work with the very best designers and architects.

One of the more recent restaurants to join his portfolio is Cha Cha Moon, a noodle bar that offers particularly quick and cheap food. The first restaurant was in Soho, but for the second, tucked away in a not particularly well-known or busy shopping centre in London's Bayswater, Yau managed to coax Japanese superstar architect Kengo Kuma on board, as well as Sake No Hana, an ultra-luxurious Japanese restaurant in Mayfair. Typical of Kuma's work, both restaurants combine traditional Japanese architectural approaches with innovative structures and materials.

Cha Cha Moon comes as a visual surprise after the empty wide expanse of the shopping centre. Despite the large glass front to the concourse, it presents itself as warm and inviting. 'Our aim was to create an endless cavern with bamboos,' explains Kuma. 'In contrast to our Great Bamboo Wall in China, where we used the bamboos vertically, in this project the bamboos are horizontal in order to make a section (or a profile) of the cavern. Mirrors were placed at both ends so that the space would be as seamless as noodles. A cave is "the other" roof indoors. Our fundamental approach towards architecture is to provide a space with a roof, not by a wall.'

The bamboo poles that straddle and define the space are 6 cm (2$^1/_2$ in) thick, and conceal the spot lighting and ducting. To keep the bamboo from cracking, every few minutes hidden humidifiers gently squirt a misty spray of water onto them, creating an unusual effect for the diners eating their noodles below. If the form of the bamboo poles subliminally referenced the noodles (as well as Asia, of course) their choice, points out Kuma, was also in harmony with the concept of a restaurant using very simple ingredients to create something of high quality.

The steel benches accompanying the long shared tables are made from steel plates that are 32 mm (1$^1/_4$ in) thick, folded says Kuma, 'like origami'. They manage to seem both sturdy and yet as delicate and exciting as the rest of the fit-out.

Noodle-like forms are used for the light-hearted logo, which keeps up the Pan-Asian theme in its typography, suggestive of Thai script. The logo is presented in a giant dotted version on the large glass panes of the restaurant's front.

Despite its beauty, the restaurant soon fell prey to the recession and also suffered because of its slightly out-of-the-way location, and sadly closed within months of opening.

3

3 Fastidious attention to detail allowed every aspect, from the suspended bamboo poles through to specially designed tables and chair as well as the open kitchen, to contribute to the exquisite feel of the restaurant.

4 View from the shopping concourse into the restaurant through the glass front wall, on which the restaurant's distinctive logo is printed large.

WAKU-WAKU

Designers
**IPPOLITO FLEITZ GROUP**
Branding
**PAJAMA**
Graphics
**BIANCA LOCKER**
Size
**135 sq m (1453 sq ft)**
Date
**2009**
Location
**HAMBURG, GERMANY**

**SUSHI AND NOODLE BARS**

1 Eccentric detailing breaks up the restaurant which is dominated by the magenta identity devised by Pajama.

2 An eclectic collection of seating was sourced from eBay and partially painted in the restaurant's trademark magenta.

3 Isometric drawing of the restaurant, showing how the narrow space extends

2

**'WAKU-WAKU'S WACKY WHOLEFOOD**-Wok-Wonder Works Worldwide'. This is the slogan adorning the wall of this unusual, ecological fast food joint in the middle of Hamburg.

Waku-Waku's founders, Pascal Le Pellec, Gregor Wöltje and André Lacroix of Good Restaurants AG, all had fast food experience of a very different kind as they had all occupied very senior roles with Burger King in Europe. Like many others, the three saw an opportunity to provide an alternative to the multinational chains and to reconcile what had been seen as two very distant and even contradictory things – fast food and sustainability.

Their 'fast food with a conscience' concept is relatively straightforward – you order your food and get given a wooden spoon with your number and wait for the wok-fried food. Despite the Japanese name (which apparently means both fried and scared), the selection of dishes includes everything from pasta and Thai curries to German staples such as Tafelspitz. There's a five-minute wait while the organic food is prepared in a wok (where everything, even the German Wurst or Schmarrn, is cooked), which the restaurant claims is more nutritious, quick and energy-efficient than conventional European means.

# 'EVERYTHING FROM PASTA AND THAI CURRIES TO GERMAN STAPLES SUCH AS TAFELSPITZ ARE PREPARED IN A WOK.'

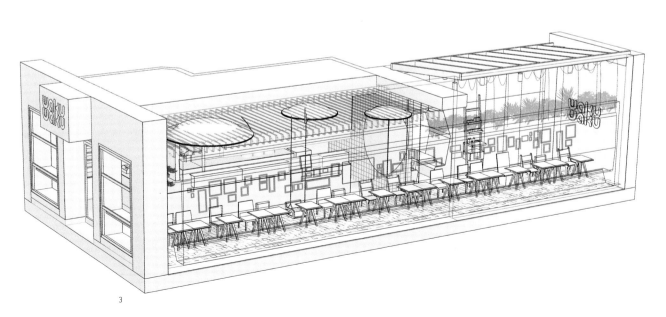

3

4

If the preparation and mixture of the dishes is unusual, so is the design. The branding, devised by Pajama in London (with additional graphics by Bianca Locker), avoids the usual aesthetic cues of eco-eateries by adopting shocking magenta as its identifying colour. The entire frontage is coloured this hue, and it is also adopted inside for the rear wall, where the branding looms large. This may seem a visual strategy more suited to the global fast food brands that its founders originally worked for, but immediately little details work to challenge that impression.

This is particularly apparent in the interior design. One of the first things you notice when you enter the restaurant is that a succession of different, secondhand chairs create the jumbled-up, irregular 'reuse' look common to environmentally-conscious interior design but rarely chosen for an otherwise slick commercial environment. To maintain cohesiveness, each of the chairs has the bottom 20 cm (8 in) painted in the trademark magenta. Acting as a 'signifier of naturalness', live plants spill out of a ledge under a glass ceiling at the rear of the space.

The design clearly creates a separation between the hi-tech kitchen, where the wok frying takes place, with its stainless steel, state-of-the-art equipment, and the lower-tech, more cosy eating area. An integrated bench with tables leads down the narrow 17-m (56-ft) deep space while on the other side there is a small alcove with a fixed table and benches, which creates an even snugger eating area. Next to this is what Waku-Waku terms its 'Pimp Station' – looking like a white ladder to nowhere, it functions as shelving to accommodate additional herbs and spices for customers who wish to give their food a bit more zing.

Three large and haphazardly-placed spoon-shaped discs hang overhead from a ribbed ceiling. Lit by LEDs, they are decorated with line drawings of the world, reflecting the range of food on offer, with a violet dot picking out the restaurant's location in Hamburg.

In keeping with the brand principles of Waku-Waku, wherever possible sustainable and Fairtrade materials were specified for the build, down to the t-shirts of the staff and the paints used to decorate. Bicycles in the brand's distinctive violet colour are used for deliveries.

Designer
**AFRODITI KRASSA**
Size
**45 sq m (485 sq ft)**
Date
**2005**
Location
**LONDON, UK**

**SUSHI AND NOODLE BARS**

'**AN INTERNATIONAL ESPIONAGE INCIDENT** has transformed Itsu into a world-famous eating place.' So read the placard in front of Itsu's branch on Piccadilly, after Russian dissident Alexander Litvinenko was radioactively poisoned during a meal inside.

After an initial wobble, the incident served only to make Itsu's restaurants famous, which is just as well, as Itsu had been transforming the presentation of fast Asian food for London's inhabitants. Suddenly, Itsu's fast food seemed quite glamorous in a James Bond kind of way, a perception that the restaurant's classy interiors were able to support.

Premium fast food is still something of a novelty, and Itsu is positioned as a slightly esoteric, quality treat, rather than an everyday destination. The chain, offering a variety of healthy, Asian-inspired dishes, is the brainchild of Julian Metcalfe, best known for the premium sandwich chain Pret a Manger. There were three Itsu restaurants (designed by Wolff Olins) already in existence, but came from an older concept – they were larger, sit-down places with food being sent round on conveyor belts.

The new fast food development began with a tiny site in Vogue House on Hanover Square, fashionably sandwiched

1

2

between upmarket Mayfair and the shops of Oxford Street. Greek-born designer Afroditi Krassa was made creative director and charged with designing every element of the store, from overhauling the branding to creating new packaging and designing the interiors. A coherent message was essential, so Krassa even worked together with the food development team to achieve this.

Designing a fast food restaurant, she says, requires particular attention to intangibles, such as how people move through the space and how quickly they are able to understand what they are meant to do. The diminutive takeaway was very much seen as a work in progress, and was developed according to the way people responded to it. Fridges, for instance, went through several different designs before everyone was happy. Unable to find anything other than white fridges, she was forced to sandblast and repaint them in black to give the required effect.

Itsu doesn't pretend to be 100 percent authentic, says Krassa, and it doesn't want to present a clichéd traditional image of Japan. She did, however, go to Japan as part of her research, looking particularly at pop culture and the way in which kitsch is used and manifests itself through popular

cartoon figures such as Hello Kitty. She also paid close attention to the Japanese packaging, particularly cosmetics, to create a feminine and modern feel.

Unlike most high-street fast food chains, each of the first stores has its own identity – the design was not conceived as a template. 'We didn't want it to feel as if every store is identical; we had to respect the specifics of the space and location,' she says. For instance, in the Hanover Square restaurant, there was a considerable amount of recycling and taking advantage of what was already there. The feature neon ceiling light replaced a large light fitting that was there before. Apart from communal branding and packaging (printed on site), certain motifs are carried across from restaurant to restaurant, such as the black-on-white panelling that references traditional Japanese paper screens.

1 Situated on Hanover Square, the first Itsu fast food outlet sought to create a distinctive premium environment that referenced modern Japan.

2 Everything from the graphics and packaging down to the fridge design was carefully overseen by the designer Afroditi Krassa.

3  Floor plan
    1) Outside seating area
    2) Inside seating
    3) Hot and cold food pick up area
    4) Tea preparation area
    5) Food preparation and storage

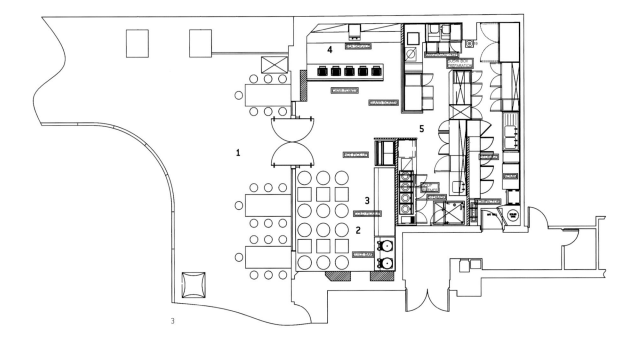

3

# 'WE DIDN'T WANT IT TO FEEL AS IF EVERY STORE IS IDENTICAL.'

4

4  Seating in the basement of the Piccadilly branch of Itsu.

5  Innovative transparent packaging was developed to allow sushi to be eaten on the go.

6  An existing neon light fitting was reworked in shocking pink.

7  View of the tea and juice bar, featuring a modern take on traditional Japanese screens.

5

6

7

ICE CREAM PARLOURS AND YOGURT BARS

1

**FROLICK**

Designers
**ASYLUM**
Size
**65 sq m (700 sq ft)**
Date
**2008**
Location
**SINGAPORE**

**ICE CREAM PARLOURS
AND YOGURT BARS**

**ORIGINATING IN CALIFORNIA, THE** craze for frozen yogurt quickly travelled around the world, including to Singapore. Asylum, a local creative agency, was approached to design the entire package for Singapore's first frozen yogurt bar, from the website and graphics to the interiors of the outlets themselves.

'The client's original idea was for it to be called Banarama, and for the design to be full of very healthy images with pictures of fruit and so on,' recounts Chris Lee, the creative director and founder of Asylum. 'We completely changed the brief after doing research which found that the target audience of 16–25 year olds wanted to buy frozen yogurt because it was fun, not because it was healthy.' This message has even translated into the yogurts that the bar sells, which come with colourful toppings such as oreo cookies and marshmallow.

So a new, more lighthearted name, Frolick, was chosen and a brand developed that would be 'politically incorrect, with added sexiness and naughtiness', he says. When faced with this edgy, anti-establishment vision 'the client was shocked but agreed,' adds Lee. Using a campaign-like approach that built on his background in advertising, Lee says that once the basic brand attributes were settled, all the collateral design, including the packaging and website (done in-house, as was everything else), proved to be relatively straightforward.

The Frolick brand's principle expression was in the button or badge. The idea was that the actual badges — expressing cheeky sentiments such as 'we stay hard longer', 'lick it!' and 'size does matter' — could be used as promotional items given away each time a new Frolick is opened, with the intention that they would become collectibles. The slogans are also used to decorate the stores' frontages.

The badges feature as a motif used throughout the design, from the packaging to the interiors, where they form the decorative lynchpin of the bright, even loud, stores. The shiny white interiors (including a white epoxy floor) have the button badges inserted in a wall in decorative swirls, while some of the stores have a wall seemingly made out of slices taken out of gargantuan badges (made of powder coated metal). White furniture (specified by the client rather than the designers) doesn't get in the way of the effect.

Loyalty schemes are common in coffee bars and places such as this, but, rather than the usual 'stamp on a card',

Asylum developed a more involved loyalty promotion, playing to the 'sexy' stance it has evolved for the brand: customers are given a little dating booklet, which gets stamped every time a purchase is made. The original outlet proved popular and was quickly followed by three others, also in Singapore.

1  Badges bearing cheeky slogans were made central to the brand, and one wall of the yogurt bar features powder coated metal panels seemingly sliced out of giant badges.

2  Shiny white walls, floor and furniture enables the graphics to create maximum impact.

2

3 Floor plan
  1) Entrance
  2) Display fridge
  3) Cashier
  4) Yogurt machines
  5) Storage areas

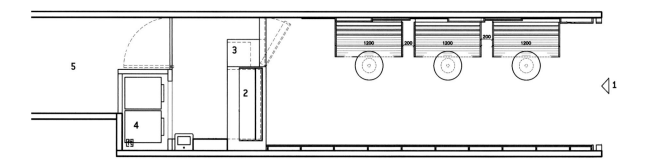

3

# 'WE FOUND THE TARGET AUDIENCE WANTED TO BUY FROZEN YOGURT BECAUSE IT WAS FUN, NOT BECAUSE IT WAS HEALTHY.'

4

**tangysweet**

**TANGYSWEET**

Designers
**KUBE ARCHITECTURE**
Size
93 sq m (1000 sq ft)
Date
2008
Location
**WASHINGTON, DC, USA**

**ICE CREAM PARLOURS
AND YOGURT BARS**

1  The view from the street shows
   off TangySweet as a radical and
   minimal space more like a night
   club than a yogurt bar.

2  Perspective drawing showing the
   U-shaped lightbox ribs that are the
   design's central conceit.

**WITH PULSATING LIGHTING MORE** akin to a conceptual art installation or nightclub, TangySweet is a frozen yogurt bar with a difference. 'We like to refer to it as a yogurt lounge,' says Janet Bloomberg of Kube Architects, who designed it.

TangySweet is located in the Dupont Circle, one of Washington, DC's liveliest and most cosmopolitan neighbourhoods. Its owner, Los Angeles-based Aaron Gordon, saw the yogurt craze gripping the West Coast and realized there was scope to introduce it to Washington, DC, where he had grown up.

Gordon approached Kube Architects to design TangySweet, wanting 'something that wouldn't look like a chain, something cutting edge and funky.' The location he had earmarked was a dark, dingy space, with no natural light, recalls Bloomberg. So the idea was hatched of making lighting the lead design element, and keeping the space clean and minimal.

The result is a pared-down design, very much in contrast with the busy designs of rivals, which Bloomberg believed had too much going on. The 'lightboxes', a series of U-shaped ribs, dominate the space, functioning as tables and, of course, as light sources.

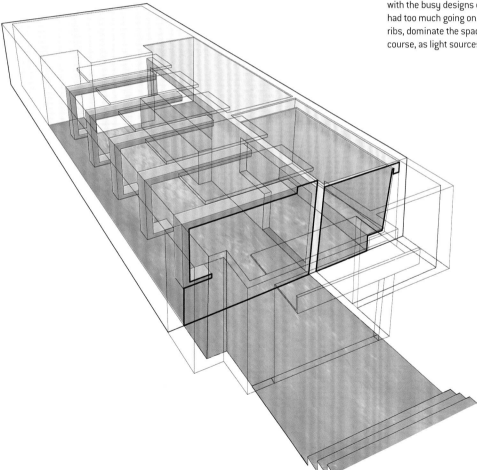

2

3 Floor plan.

4&5 The lightboxes contain
programmed LED lighting that
change colour every 45 seconds.

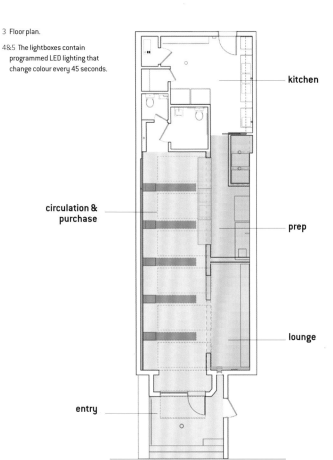

kitchen

circulation &
purchase

prep

lounge

entry

3

## 'THE OWNER WANTED SOMETHING THAT WOULDN'T LOOK LIKE A CHAIN, SOMETHING CUTTING EDGE AND FUNKY.'

'The lightboxes are programmed to change colour every 45 seconds or so,' she explains. 'We didn't want it to be so fast that it looked like a light show, but we wanted to make sure it was perceived during the short visit a typical customer would make to buy a yogurt. So it's subtle, but you definitely realize the colours have changed.' A variety of different 'colour scenes', including a simple single colour scheme, are available at the push of a button.

Taking inspiration from the name TangySweet, the architects mixed smooth and rough surfaces. Viroc walls (concealing a steel structure needed to support the lightboxes), a roughly finished concrete floor and a simple wooden counter area are set against the recycled resin lightboxes and the glass wall. Wall-mounted vinyl graphics, developed by the architects in conjunction with the owner, provide another textural contrast.

The resulting nightclub-like vibe was intentional. TangySweet gets very busy at night, staying open into the early hours on weekends, when the lighting scheme comes into its own. Due to cost considerations, the LED lighting elements inside the lightboxes (crafted by Lightblocks) were restricted to two – one in each corner, with their

effectiveness stretched by the use of mirrors. Technical assistance came from lighting consultants George Sexton Associates. The ceiling was layered, seemingly woven in an effect designed to increase the perception of height in the long narrow space. A single recessed fluorescent light provides the complementary lighting. Off to one side is a slightly more relaxed lounge area, and a small outside area is cleverly integrated with the interior.

4

5

133

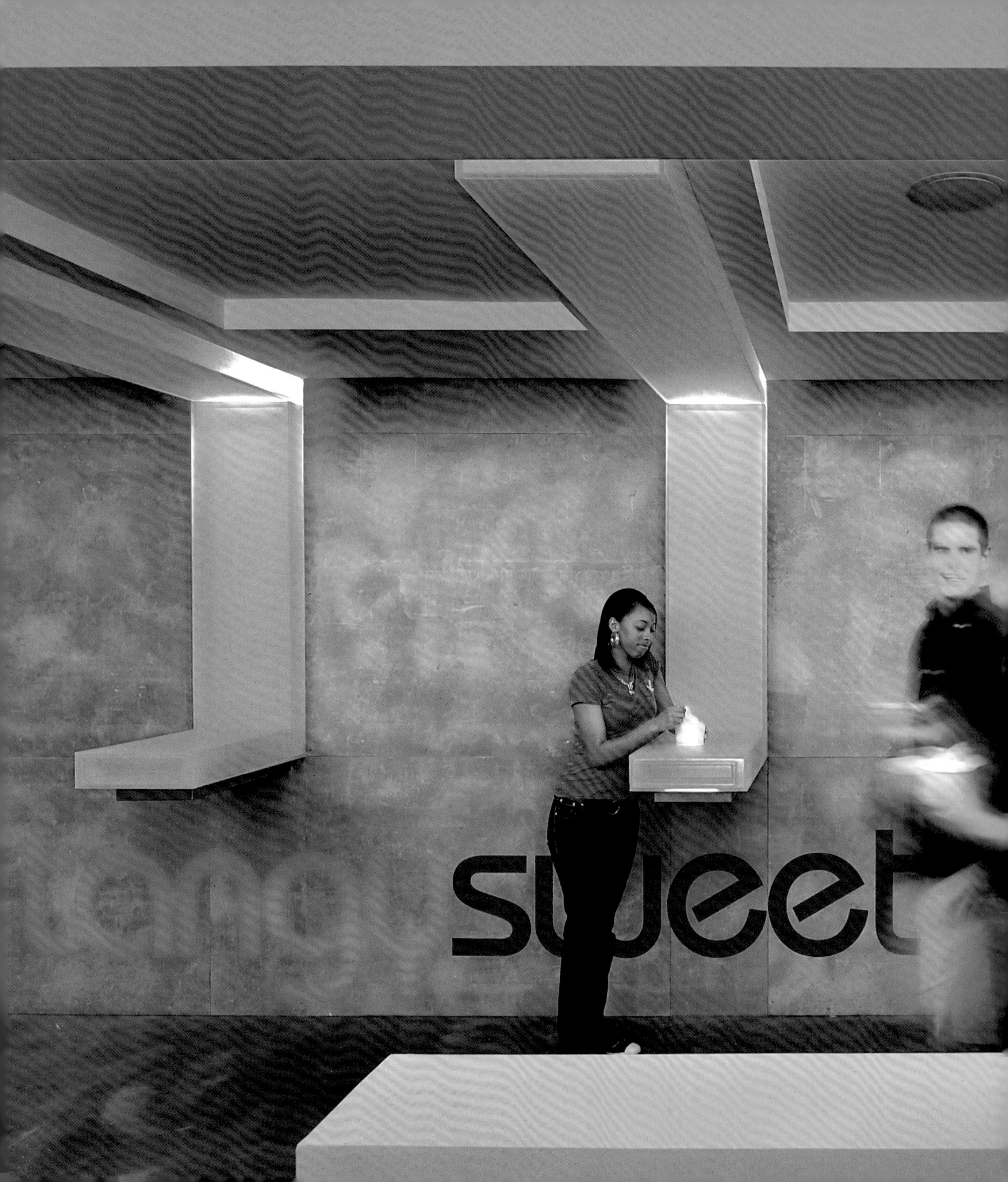
sweet

6 As well as functioning as a lighting installation, the lightboxes also serve as impromptu tables for customers wanting to eat their frozen yogurt on the premises.

Interior and lighting
design
**CINIMOD STUDIO**
Branding and graphics
**ICO DESIGN**
Size
**20 sq m/40 sq m (215 sq
ft/430 sq ft)**
Date
**2009**
Location
**LONDON, UK**

SNOG

**SNOG**™
Pure Frozen Yogurt

1 A spectacular light installation made up of 700 suspended balls means that Snog cuts a distinctive dash after dark in the visually busy environment of London's Soho.

2 Section of the yogurt bar showing public area together with private storage and preparation areas.

**SNOG IS HOW FROZEN** yogurt arrived in England in the summer of 2008, introduced by a Colombian architect, Pablo Uribe, and his US-born business partner Rob Baines. They wanted it to be a very British yet lively interpretation of the yogurt craze, with ambitious plans for expansion.

An extrovert brand identity and tone of voice was developed by Ico Design ('put snow and yogurt together, and what you get is Snog') and work began on creating emotive and experiential spaces where the frozen yogurt could be bought and consumed. While he didn't design the space himself, Uribe took a very close interest and brought on board young designer Dominic Harris, who had just set up Cinimod Studio after working in the studios of Future Systems and Jason Bruges.

The first store opened in South Kensington. The 20 sq m (215 sq ft) space is designed to 'evoke the feeling of a perfect never ending summer', says Harris. It all takes place under a ceiling that functions as a 'digital sky', programmed to continually change throughout the day, much like the British weather. The 'grass' underfoot is actually a photographic vinyl floor, and stylized meadow flowers designed by Ico adorn the walls, which are made of glass.

SNOG

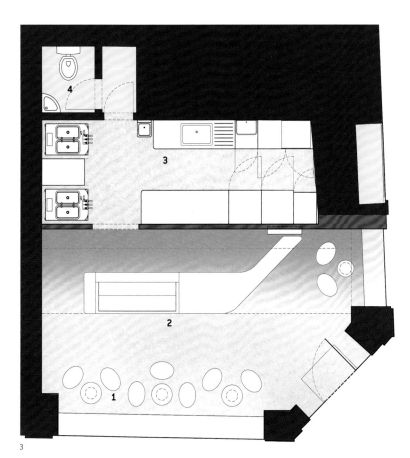

3 Floor plan
  1) Public seating area
  2) Main service counter
  3) Kitchen and preparation area
  4) Toilet

4 View of the curved Corian counter
  and Shitake stools by Marcel
  Wanders on a surreal vinyl floor
  that appears to be grass.

3

Seating is by way of little mushrooms, or the plastic stools called Shitake designed by Marcel Wanders for Moroso.

A second store, opened in the middle of Soho, managed the unlikely feat of outshining its predecessor. Despite being crowded by the neon of strip joints and gay bars, Snog is able to stand out, largely due to its highly adventurous lighting. Many aspects of the previous store are carried over, including the 'grass' floor, but the 'sky' becomes the space's salient feature.

'Instead of having a flat ceiling I really felt that we should exploit the ceiling heights we had and instead create something more "volumetric" and bubbling,' says Harris. 'People now describe the ceiling as effervescent, which I really like.' Over 700 of the specially designed light fittings were produced. Each frosted glass globe hanging from the ceiling is individually controlled and capable, thanks to its LED internals, of millions of colours. The whole installation was programmed and commissioned by Harris.

The shiny white counter and window seat are bespoke and were made using proprietary Hi-Macs acrylic. The pink paint is partly fluorescent, adding to the bold and very urban feel of the design, but with more than a hint of retro. Harris accepts that in many ways the design uses approaches that are more common to the world of fashion than food.

An essential part of the concept was that the shops should not be static, but continually evolving. While the lighting installation goes some way to achieving this with its constant changes in mood and hue, the walls are regularly given over to guest artists or illustrators commissioned by Ico Design through the Young Creatives Network. They are allowed to leave their mark on the interior and exterior of the restaurants, until their work is replaced by that of another artist. For the interior, the designs are applied to the glass walls in the form of vinyl cut-outs.

4

'PEOPLE NOW DESCRIBE THE CEILING AS EFFERVESCENT,
WHICH I REALLY LIKE.'

5 View from outside of the original South Kensington Snog, which features a ceiling that relies on thousands of programmed LEDs to emulate clouds moving across an English summer sky.

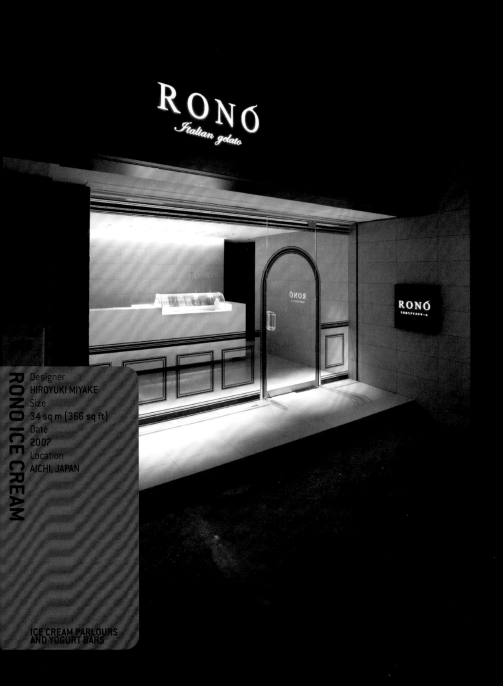

RONO
*Italian gelato*

**RONO ICE CREAM**

Designer
HIROYUKI MIYAKE
Size
34 sq m (366 sq ft)
Date
2007
Location
AICHI, JAPAN

ICE CREAM PARLOURS
AND YOGURT BARS

1  The austere neoclassical exterior
   of the Rono ice cream parlour as it
   appears at night.

2  Floor plan.

DIMINUTIVE YET AUSTERE, THE Rono Ice Cream parlour is a surreal temple that fulfils its task with the utmost seriousness. Its designer, Hiroyuki Miyake, conceived it as a place where getting and eating an ice cream could – rather than being a flippant, self-indulgent activity – become a dream-like act. Like the Madeleine biscuit that evoked memories in Marcel Proust's *Remembrance of Things Past*, the eating of an Italian ice cream becomes the trigger for leisurely recollections and associations.

Miyake drew on recollections of holidays spent in Italy for the design of the parlour, taking as a starting point a row of houses along a city street. Rather than interpreting this realistically, he used the memory as a starting point to distil these very pared down, neoclassical cues that hint at Italy.

'I wanted to choose only one kind of tile for the wall and the floor to act as the background,' explains Miyake. 'This tile was to have no colour, no texture, no reflection and no character, and was to be used inside and out. There are two reasons why I used a muted colour palette; one was to enhance the colour of the ice cream itself, the other was because I wanted to express the unrealistic element like a monochromatic dream.'

The stark simplicity of the space makes the mirror at one end of the parlour more effective. 'I wanted to express a mysterious atmosphere like Alice's adventures in Wonderland,' says Miyaki. A framed, mirrored display within the mirror-wall adds to the effect. Items such as apples, changing regularly, are lit mysteriously in a design that seeks to break down distinctions between reality and non-reality. The nameplate too suggests a jewellery shop or luxury boutique, and belies the parlour's unassuming location in an apartment block in Ichinomiya, near Nagoya in Aichi Prefecture.

The austerity is broken only by the bright colours of the 40 different flavours of ice cream. These are rotated, with some of more popular flavours served every day while others are sold as they come into season.

Kitchen

Shop

2

Entrance

# 'I WANTED TO EXPRESS THE UNREALISTIC ELEMENT LIKE A MONOCHROMATIC DREAM.'

3 A framed mirror unit allows for a rotating display of fresh fruit.

4 The muted colours and surfaces of the parlour contrast with the bright colours of the ice cream.

5 Detail showing the refined
presentation of the served
ice cream.

6 A wall of mirrors creates a
disconcerting Alice in Wonderland-
like spatial confusion.

5

BURGER BARS, CAFETERIAS AND OTHER SMALL RESTAURANTS

1

Designers
McDONALD'S EUROPE
AND PHILIPPE AVANZI,
MANAGING DIRECTOR OF
ATELIER ARCHANGE
Size
VARIOUS
Date
2006 ONWARDS
Location
ACROSS EUROPE

**McDONALD'S**

BURGER BARS,
CAFETERIAS AND OTHER
SMALL RESTAURANTS

**'WE WANT THE CUSTOMER** to see a difference; we want to stop them in their tracks and to make them return again and again to the destination,' explains Isabelle Guyé, a project manager at McDonald's European Restaurant Development & Design Studio.

McDonald's is, of course, synonymous with fast food, and its incredibly successful global chain of restaurants has become a conduit for criticism of all that is wrong with our atomized, unhealthy, artificial and unsustainable culture. Having in the past taken an aggressive stance on these issues, McDonald's has more recently sought to alter perceptions of its food and practices and present a healthier and more sustainable face to the world. Part of this radical overhaul involved a genuinely startling transformation of the design of its restaurants, beginning in Europe.

Looking tired, these restaurants had exemplified the 'cookie cutter' approach to environmental branding that visually typifies contemporary globalization. Wherever you looked, from Sweden to Syria, every McDonald's looked the same. The shiny red surfaces of this standardized design increasingly came across as cheap and cynical. But in 2006 this began to change, as McDonald's rolled out a series of new designs in Europe developed together with its external creative director, Philippe Avanzi, and his design studio Atelier Archange.

'During the discovery phase, it was necessary to "shout" our brand. Today, the recognition allows us to "whisper" it,' Guyé says. 'Everybody knows McDonald's and it is a real chance for a brand. Being "simply McDonald's", more integrated, sustainable, responsible is our credo. We definitely want to differentiate ourselves from the streetscape and we are progressing on our journey to move from "fast food" to "good food fast".'

Various different versions of the new design are presented to franchised restaurants in a detailed catalogue, and they are strongly encouraged to adopt one in its entirety according to cost, location and customer profile. While it was envisaged as an evolving and flexible program, eight individual (though subtly connected) designs were made available. These include LIM/Fresh, which is presented as the design that most reflects the contemporary expression of the McDonald's brand. Lime-green walls and lampshades mix with iconic postwar furniture and oversized graphics of fresh food. In LIM/Edge, aimed at an older audience, more muted

"autumnal" tones, combining wood furniture and finely striped graphics with directional lighting, attempt a more sophisticated atmosphere. Another, Eternity, is a sumptuous and more glamorous design that heavily references Art Deco.

Most noticeable is the change in materials – rather than the shiny ostentatious plastic that once characterized McDonald's, wood is now prevalent, both in exterior latticework and the dividing screens inside. The specification of instantly recognizable (and conspicuously expensive) designs by Arne Jacobson and Charles and Ray Eames allows the teenager munching on a Big Mac to experience a sense of luxury and suggests authenticity and sophistication to passersby – two qualities with which McDonald's had not previously been associated.

However, a disagreement between McDonald's and Danish manufacturer Fritz Hansen stopped the supply of the classic furniture. While this put a stop to one of the most conspicuous elements of the redesign, the overall new design direction meant that McDonald's restaurants would never look the same again.

1 Making shiny red plastic a thing of the past, the new McDonald's look, as is evident in London's Holborn restaurant, suggests new values with the use of subdued colours and wood on the outside and a more expensive looking interior

2 The LIM/Fresh concept, distinguished by its use of lime green furniture and lighting, together with wood slats to articulate different areas.

3 Oversized imagery of fresh fruit
and vegetables on the walls signal
McDonald's wish to acknowledge
healthy eating concerns, while
curved seating and large
lampshades provide a new,
more luxurious feel.

4 The Eternity concept is intended
to evoke the design heritage of Art
Deco America with its connotations
of sumptuous glamour.

'WE ARE PROGRESSING ON OUR JOURNEY TO MOVE FROM "FAST FOOD" TO "GOOD FOOD FAST".'

3

4

5 The more Autumnal tones of the LIM/Edge version, shown here in a McDonald's restaurant In Paris.

Designers
**HHF ARCHITECTS**
Size
**120 sq m (1292 sq ft)**
Date
**2008**
Location
**BASEL, SWITZERLAND**

**BURGER BARS, CAFETERIAS AND OTHER SMALL RESTAURANTS**

1

# 'THE WOODEN INTERNAL STRUCTURE FLOATS ABOVE THE ORIGINAL CONCRETE, AND IS ONLY FIXED IN A FEW LOCATIONS.'

**AT FIRST SIGHT THIS** could be taken for a rather upmarket restaurant in a capital city, but it is in fact the cafeteria for the pupils of a school in Basel, Switzerland. Located on the outskirts of the city, the Kirschgarten Gymnasium wanted to offer its students a wholesome and quality alternative to roaming the local streets and frequenting fast food restaurants in their lunch breaks.

The local authority also decreed that the new *mensa* (Latin for 'table' and the common term for school and university restaurants in central and southern Europe) should be shared with a neighbouring school, the De-Wette-Schule. They wanted a space that would work as an informal social space that the pupils would naturally gravitate towards, as well as functioning as a proper cafeteria with on-site catering.

The only area that would be easily accessible to the pupils of both schools was the rather austere, concrete-slabbed foyer of the Kirschgarten Gymnasium. This, however, did present a problem because the structure, like the rest of the school, was a listed building constructed in 1957 and designed by celebrated local architect Hans Benno Bernoulli.

HHF architects, also based in Basel, decided on an

2

unusual approach, with the support of the local planning officials. As the architects were not allowed to tamper with the structure or make any intervention that was not reversible, they designed an elaborate internal skin made of plywood, pine and MDF. The sections are compared by the architects to ribbons, which subliminally connect the interior with the space outside. This wooden internal structure floats above the original concrete, and is only fixed in a few locations. If required, every single element of the new design could be ripped out and the structure returned to its former status.

The new wooden interior is joined by large wooden steps leading up to the former foyer, which also fulfills the council's wish for informal casual seating and integrates the cafeteria with the courtyard playground in front. A retractable canopy was also devised to cover these external steps during bad weather. The foyer itself, once an open, windswept area, is now protected from the elements with glazing on steel supports that are discreetly hidden behind the original concrete pillars, retaining the original slim-pillared effect.

The working kitchen is included in this wooden structure-within-a-structure. The layered wood panelling of the space is treated to an unusually subtle colour scheme devised in association with a local artist, Gido Wiederkehr. Eschewing the bright colours usually chosen for schools, the wood is painted in three similar shades of grey, which gently articulate the different panel elements and break up the space. The choice of grey also references the concrete of the original structure. HHF Architects also designed bespoke benches, seating and tables for the cafeteria. Their dark wood reinforces a sense of quality and permanence, and they are offset nicely by the grey wood and concrete backdrop.

The kitchen is run by a local restaurant group, and serves fresh, healthy food that is prepared daily, but the students can also bring their own packed lunches and consume them in the cafeteria.

1 The Kirschgarten Cafeteria seen lit after dark from the school playground.

2 A retractable canopy hangs over wooden steps that create a sociable connection with the playground outside.

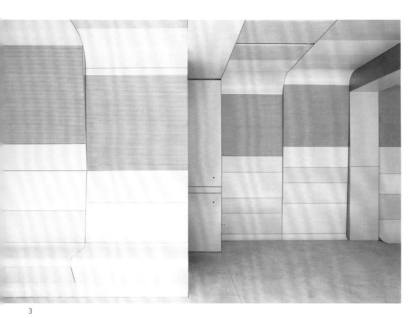

3

3 The internal wood panels are painted in three shades of grey in a colour scheme devised by artist Gido Wiederkehr, eschewing the bright colour schemes normally selected for school environments.

4&5 The pupils are treated to a cafeteria that is unusually restrained and refined.

4

5

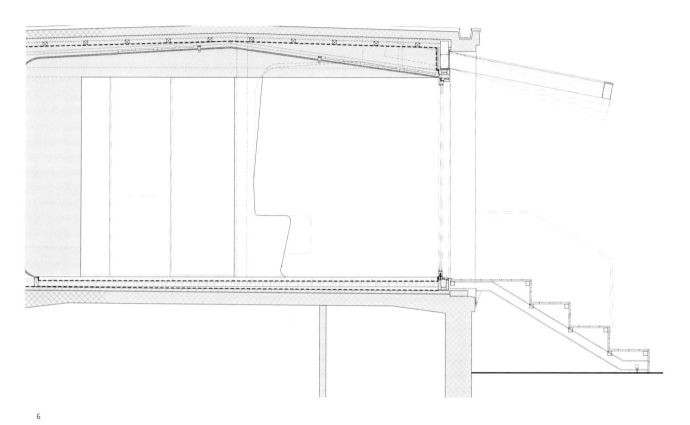

6 Section showing the way in
which the wooden structure has
been inserted within the existing
concrete pavilion with minimal
structural intervention.

7 The warmth of the bespoke dark
wood tables and stools contrasts
with the grey of the concrete and
interior wood panelling.

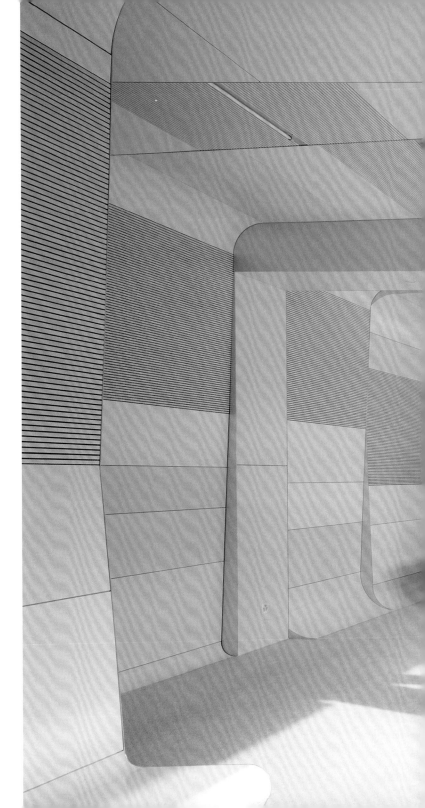

Designers
**AB ROGERS DESIGN**
Graphics
**PRALINE AND DOMINIC
ROBSON (INTERACTIVE)**
Size
**105 sq m (1130 sq ft)
excluding toilets and
service area**
Date
**2009
KETTERING, UK**

**BURGER BARS,
CAFETERIAS AND OTHER
SMALL RESTAURANTS**

1 Floor plan
   1) Entrance lobby
   2) Main seating area
   3) Lobby
   4) Disabled toilet
   5) Female toilet
   6) Male toilet
   7) Servery

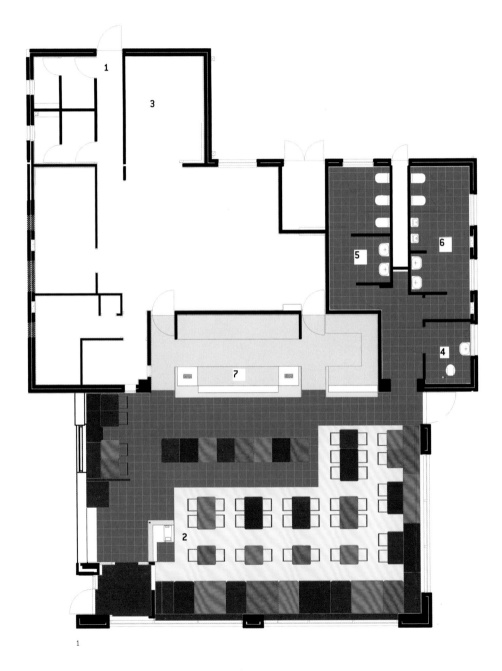

1

2 Illuminated outdoor sign featuring
new graphics and identity created
by Praline.

2

'PEOPLE JUST COME IN TO USE THE
TOILET AND DON'T SPEND A PENNY IN
THE RESTAURANT, SO WE HAD TO FIND A
WAY TO CAPTURE THESE PEOPLE AND MAKE
THEM STAY.'

**LITTLE CHEF IS A** British institution. Founded in the 1950s,
the chain of roadside cafés provides cheap and informal
food to travelling families or business people on the road.
Like other brands such as Wimpy, Little Chef took American
influences – the 1950s roadside diner, for instance – and
domesticated them to appeal to British tastes. The full
English breakfast was its signature dish. While very popular
in its heyday, a lack of investment and modernization had
seen the chain's cheap and cheerful image take a battering,
and Little Chef was widely perceived as languishing in the
1970s, both in terms of its décor and its food.

In 2007, however, Little Chef was rescued from
administration by a private equity firm, and its new chief
executive sought ways to reinject the fun and positive
associations that the restaurants once had. To celebrate
its 50-year anniversary, Heston Blumenthal, one of the
country's best-known Michelin-starred chefs, was brought
onboard to overhaul the menu for its restaurant in Popham,
and the whole process of reinvigoration was filmed as part of
a major television documentary.

Blumenthal brought in Ab Rogers to redesign the
restaurant's tired interior, and the promise was made that if

3 The seating areas are divided
between the more traditional
tables and chairs, aimed at
families, and the bar arrangement
for solitary travellers. Ceiling tiles
evoke the seaside sky.

the new design and menu was a success it would be rolled out across the chain's other restaurants. Like Blumenthal with restaurants, Ab Rogers is usually associated with the top end of the design market, with well-known work for luxury brands such as Commes des Garçons.

'We developed the brief closely with Heston,' explains Rogers. 'We wanted to create a new Little Chef that would not alienate existing clients but that would also celebrate the future. We then got really excited by the whole thing as we began to do research.'

The result was a very colourful and playful design, which Rogers describes as 'nostalgic values from traditional places like eel and pie shops with a bit of an influence from American diners, pushed into the future with high-tech printing and an interactive installation in the toilets.'

Little Chef suffers from a problem common to other roadside cafés. 'About half the people just come in to use the toilet and don't spend a penny in the restaurant, so we had to find a way to capture these people and make them stay,' says Rogers. Working with Dominic Robson, a humorous interactive environment was devised for the toilets to encourage people to stay and have a coffee or a bite to eat.

The aroma of coffee is pumped into the corridor near the toilets, and there is a recording of pots and pans being clanked and people shouting, or what Rogers describes as 'authentic kitchen din'. An infrared sensor detects when someone approaches a urinal or toilet, and various songs about food begin to play, sung by classic English comedians such as Spike Milligan and Morecambe and Wise.

Little Chef's branding was given the once over by graphic designers Praline together with Ab Rogers, and a new colour spectrum was introduced for the iconic figure. These reds, a classic feature of 1950s' diners, dominate the interiors of the redesigned restaurants through their use on the tables and vinyl seating. Standard ceiling tiles are enlivened with images of seagulls flying under a blue sky, blue mosaic tiles are used for the counters and simple white ceramic tiling in much of the rest of the space. It was important for Rogers that the new restaurants appear bright and clean. 'They originally suggested carpet for the floor – which would have been criminal,' he says.

3

4

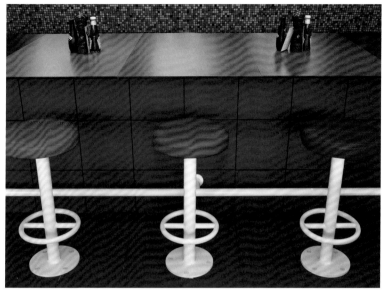

5

6

4 Ab Rogers seated at the central canteen table.

5 Contemporary mosaic tiling contrasts with the retro red vinyl covered bar stools.

6 Colourful tiling in the bathroom area contains little drawings and text relating to food, all in the interests of detaining motorists who might otherwise simply use to facilities rather than buy any refreshments or food.

7 Ab Rogers washing his hands in the interactive toilet area, in which songs about food are played when an infrared sensor detects the presence of a visitor.

7

Designers
**MUT-ARCHITECTURE AND
LE POTAGER DESIGN**
Size
**200 sq m (2153 sq ft)**
Date
**2009**
Location
**PARIS, FRANCE**

1 The restaurant quite literally connects with the outside by means of a curved bench table that seems to pass through the wall.

2 Plan showing how the modular table snakes in and out of the restaurant.

# 'ALL VISITORS WANT TO SIT AT THE PICNIC TABLE.'

**IN THE 12TH ARRONDISSEMENT** of Paris you will find a typically idiosyncratic building by Frank Gehry. Built in 1994 as the American Centre, it had been standing empty until the French Government purchased it to house the national film archive and theatre. The Cinémathèque Française opened its doors in 2005 and four years later got the café it deserved.

'There had been a restaurant there but it was closed – it was dark, badly designed and basically didn't work at all,' says John Mascaro of Mut-Archicture. He and his partner Eléonore Morant, together with old friends Le Potager Design, won a mini competition by restaurateur client Hughes Piketty to reinvent the space, now to be known as Restaurant 51.

The brief was simple – to create an eating space that would connect with the park outside. The designers chose to interpret this literally, conceiving a picnic table that seamlessly snakes in and out of the space: appearing to go straight through the glass walls, it ties the dark interior with the Parc de Bercy outside. 'We wanted to make a playful space, to create something interesting,' says Mascaro.

The budget was very tight, as was the timeframe. The entire build and fit-out took only six weeks, with both sets of designers on-site for most of the time, making items

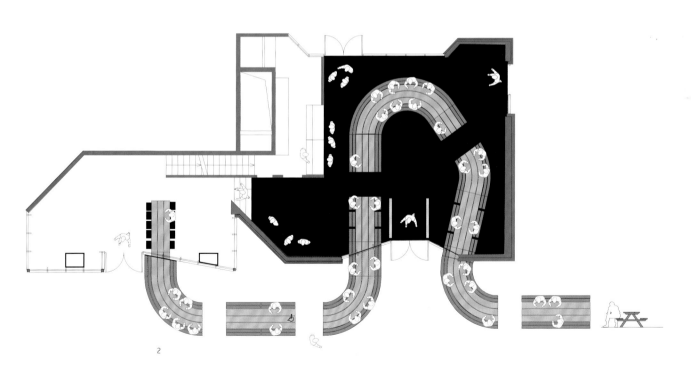

2

ENTRÉE →

3 The table's curves were achieved by clamping rather than the more usual technique of steam bending by Swiss specialists, while the oversize window graphics were inherited from an earlier design and kept at the wish of the client.

4

5

4 The snaking table features a dip to store menus or books before seemingly passing through the glass wall to the outside.

5 Chandeliers were created from inexpensive fittings sourced from New York's Chinatown.

6

7

themselves. The table was carefully fabricated from pine by Swiss specialists Kunstbetrieb, with whom Mascaro had worked previously in New York. Mut and Kunstbetrieb devised a process using glue and clamps to create the complicated bends in the wood without using steam. Some 40 m (131 ft) long, the table's modular construction allows it to be moved around and reconfigured if required.

The rest of the furniture was sourced from flea markets and second-hand shops. This was then dismantled, hacked up and generally punished before being reassembled for the food display. It was painted the same black as the room, and the main counter is supported on a set of seven scattered pairs of filled-in fishing boots rather than conventional legs for a discreetly surreal effect. Similarly, the lighting was improvised at little cost – the ad hoc chandeliers were constructed inexpensively from simple fittings found in New York's Chinatown.

A second white room was intended for private functions or for more elderly visitors who might not enjoy the informality of the snaking picnic table. But in reality all visitors want to sit at the picnic table, say the designers. The idea of one white room and one black room was set out

in the brief, but the space is intersected by a mezzanine housing the library, which the designers chose to paint a vibrant red.

The client's initial idea included a facility where hampers containing a readymade picnic could be rented. These could be consumed either at the picnic table or out in the park on chairs supplied by the restaurant. By day there is a canteen service, while by night the space becomes a restaurant with table service.

The window graphics, showing stills from pioneering early French films, were already in situ and had to be worked around. Gehry's architecture, too, was very much of its time, but the designers didn't let this stand in their way. 'We wanted to set up a contrast with the architecture,' says Mascaro, and the swirling, deconstructive picnic table is in its own way every bit as eccentric as the architecture it twists in and out of, while providing an unusually effective and entertaining eating space.

Designer
**MARTÍ GUIXÉ**
Size
**18.5 sq m (200 sq ft)**
Date
**2004**
Location
**BARCELONA, SPAIN**

CAMPER

FoodBALL

COMPLEMENTS/SIDE DISHES
0.60€   0.95€
HARD-BOILED EGG
0.65€
INCA BISCUITS
1.25€
SOUP OF THE DAY   FRESH AND SEASONAL FRUIT

SALSES/SAUCES
0.95€
WHITE MISO   COCO AND CURRY
SOYA AND GINGER

**BURGER BARS, CAFETERIAS AND OTHER SMALL RESTAURANTS**

DULCES/BOMBONES   DULCES/SWEET BALLS
7.95€
DATILES DATILS DATE   ALGARROBA GARROFA CAROB BEAN
SORBETES DE TEMPORADA SORBETS DE TEMPORADA SEASONAL SORBETS
2.25€

1 Main serving counter of the Barcelona FoodBALL restaurant featuring the graphics of Martí Guixé on the rear wall.

2 Perspective drawing showing the ramped seating area of the eating space, conceived as an area that would blur the distinction between inside and out.

2

**THE COLLABORATION OF CATALAN** Martí Guixé and Mallorcan shoe brand Camper has become widely known and respected, and successive concept stores have challenged retail conventions and made designers and other retail brands sit up, take notice, and often copy them.

Camper FoodBALL was an attempt to bring this same innovative and fresh thinking to fast food. The idea was to maintain the brand values of the Camper shoe but see how they could be transferred to an edible product and a very different form of retailing. It also allowed Guixé to unite his experience in designing retail spaces with his ongoing interest in 'food design', the subject of many projects of different kinds that investigate our relationship with food and its construction.

The main food itself was novel – a fried ball of rice with various optional fillings, somewhat akin to the arancino, or 'little orange' rice-based street food of southern Italy. Guixé influenced the food concept but he was not involved in the development of it directly. 'It was developed by more than five different chefs until the definitive thing was arrived at,' he says. 'I do not know how to cook; that's why a chef is always needed.'

While the foodballs themselves may have been unusual (even though they were complemented by more usual health-food offerings such as juices), Camper FoodBALL's real innovation lay elsewhere. Guixé managed the seemingly impossible – he invented a new kind of interior eating space. Adjoining the small serving area with the counter where the little foodballs were neatly laid out was a large room with concrete steps rising to one side like a section of a stadium, or the steps leading up to a major monument from some public square. A few straw cushions indicated they were for sitting on, supported by the slightly surreal positioning of table lamps. It's a space conceived by looking at social conventions rather than the principles of interior design.

Eating spaces are normally clearly defined, but here there is something in between. It was important for Guixé that, for instance, someone could come in on their bicycle and leave it inside the space. It formalizes the little outdoor spaces colonized by tourists or office workers for lunch and takes it inside. Guixé wanted it to be familiar and alien at the same time. It was designed in order to be comfortable, so that people could see it as a place to stay and eat their food, yet not so comfortable that they would stay beyond what

3

3 The FoodBALLs were a novel food
format of a fried ball of rice with
different filling devised by a team
of chefs.

4 Cushions and lights soften the
concrete steps to make them
inviting enough for visitors to
sit and eat their food yet not so
comfortable that people would
stay any longer than necessary.

was necessary, taking up space.

'It was a takeaway, so I wanted to create a space which is not a dining room, but allowed people to eat in a informal way, like in the street. That is why there were the stairs, and people could enter inside with a bicycle. It was not really a defined space, it was not exterior, but also not an interior; at least not a typical interior for a restaurant,' he says.

It was also to be 'super-photogenic without following any conventional parameters'. 'The more photogenic it is, the more it would be in the media; the more in the media, the more it would be visited: and therefore the more successful it would be,' he says with typical frankness.

As the food on offer was healthy, organic fare, it was important that the restaurant's construction was also as sustainable as possible, and Guixé worked with specialist external architectural consultants to that end. The graphics, logo and menu were all executed in Guixé's trademark, cute hand-drawn style, much emulated by brands not wishing to seem too 'corporate'. They gently play around with the similarity between the concept's name and the game of football, which links in with the sporty feel of the brand.

The original restaurant in Barcelona was opened in 2004, and was followed two years later by another FoodBALL in Berlin's Mitte district. However, the anticipated wider roll-out didn't happen and the restaurants were eventually closed. Their idea remains as a peculiarly original take on the fast food restaurant.

4

'IT WAS NOT EXTERIOR, BUT ALSO NOT AN INTERIOR.'

# pluk

**PLUK**

Designers
TJEP.
Size
45 sq m (484 sq ft)
Date
2008
Location
HAARLEM, NETHERLANDS

**BURGER BARS,
CAFETERIAS AND OTHER
SMALL RESTAURANTS**

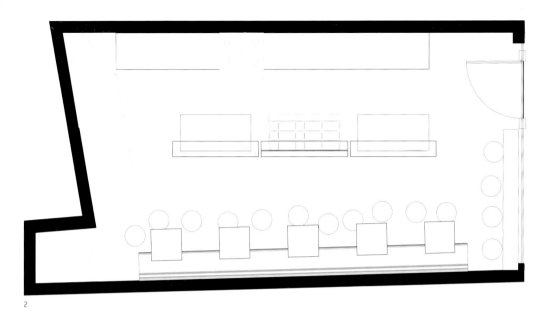

1 Colourful plastic fruit behind glass and confident graphics are intended to make Pluk a vibrant and cheerful environment.

2 Floor plan showing the straightforward layout of the diminutive café.

# 'PLASTIC FRUIT AND VEGETABLES, GROUPED BY COLOUR, SIT BEHIND TRANSLUCENT COLOURFUL GLASS COUNTERS.'

'I'M FASCINATED BY FAST food concepts as cultural phenomena. Now is a very interesting transition period, because in the eco and slow food age, fast food has to totally reinvent itself,' says Frank Tjepkema of Amsterdam-based design consultancy Tjep. So when he was approached by a couple of friends to design a small health food café and takeaway in nearby Haarlem, it was a welcome chance to explore what such a new place could look like.

A location was found right in the middle of the historic centre of Haarlem, just behind the exquisite Frans Hals Museum, and the café was christened Pluk – one of the meanings of the Dutch word *pluk* is the same as the English 'pluck', suggestive of harvest and therefore all things healthy. The idea behind Pluk was to serve fresh food, such as salads made up of ingredients selected by customers, as well as conventional health food fare and yogurts. As with many new-generation health food outlets, the owners were very keen to keep a sense of fun and not to be too puritanical about the diet – fun and 'naughty' treats were to be allowed too.

The design sought to take the two disparate elements of wholefood and fun and combine them in a single concept.

3

The result is a very colourful, cheery space that isn't afraid to be a bit 'pop'. Keen to differentiate themselves from plasticky global franchises, places such as this usually set great store by 'authenticity' and 'naturalness'; attributes that are normally translated into the design. But Tjep. steered clear of neutral, natural palettes and materials and bravely pushed the artificial to the fore. Fake plastic fruit and vegetables, grouped by colour, sit behind translucent glass counters that are printed in yellow, green and pink. The designers say they were determined that the space would not be boring and austere, and emphasize the amount of effort that went into finding a combination of colours, fruits and heights to get the desired effect.

The glass service bar and counter run almost the entire length of the small space. There is a conventional window bar-table and stools as well as a set of tables that are set in front of a pink bench accompanied by small, white plastic stools, appropriately called Happy (and manufactured by Pedrali).

Almost the only 'natural' material in the space is the matching Mikado dark wood of the tables and floor. However, Nature makes another unnatural appearance in the form of the giant vegetable and fruit graphics that punctuate the walls. These too were created by Tjep., who were responsible for all aspects of the design, including the graphics and the branding.

3 The translucent glass counter also
serves as the space's principle
decoration.

4 View over the food containers and
glass counter to the pink bench
and oversized wall graphics.

**Designers**
JONAS LINDVALL AND
MIKAEL LING FOR
LINDVALL A&D
**Lighting**
LJUS I HUS AB
**Size**
120 sq m (1292 sq ft)
60 covers
**Date**
2007
**Location**
MALMÖ, SWEDEN

**BLOOM IN THE PARK**

**BURGER BARS,
CAFETERIAS AND OTHER
SMALL RESTAURANTS**

bloom

# 'SOME 90 SQUARE METRES OF GOLD LEAF WERE USED TO DECORATE THE ENTRANCE LOBBY AND THE CORRIDOR.'

1  The restaurant is housed in a wooden Alpine hut in Pildammsparken in Malmö.

2  The gold leaf covered walls of the entrance lobby shimmer in the late afternoon sun.

**A SHORT TAXI RIDE** takes you to what seems like an Alpine hut located in the Pildammsparken, the largest park in the southern Swedish city of Malmö. The dark exterior of this unassuming structure does little to prepare you for what greets you when you go through the door at the top of the small flight of steps. Enter the restaurant and you walk into a circular entrance hall that shimmers with gold. Signalling consummate luxury to arriving diners, the gold catches the late afternoon sunlight. In total, 90 sq m (970 ft) of gold leaf were used to decorate the entrance lobby, the corridor leading off it and its concealed wardrobes.

As there wasn't much the designers, Lindvall A&D, could do to the exterior of the listed building, they chose instead to maximize the contrast with the experience inside. Jonas Lindvall explains that he sought to create an interior and most importantly, an atmosphere, that was appropriate to the fine food on offer and to the clientele. As something of a regular at the restaurant in its previous location about ten minutes away, Lindvall understood what was required – something special and unique, rather like the food. At the behest of its British owner Igi Vidal, the restaurant dispenses with the usual menu and tariff of prices to offer a very

2

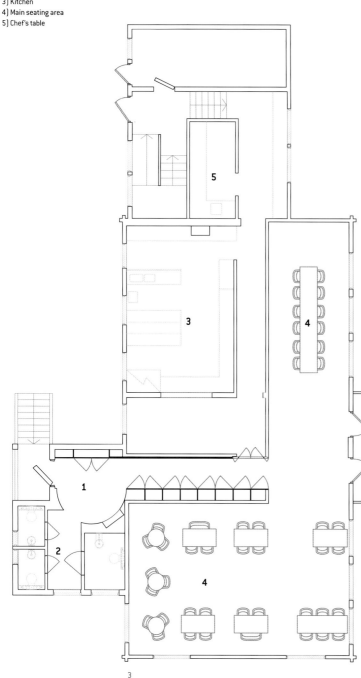

3 Floor plan
 1) Entrance lobby
 2) Toilets
 3) Kitchen
 4) Main seating area
 5) Chef's table

5

3

4

1

2

4

3

personalized dining experience. Lindvall's design seeks to produce a similarly bespoke interior.

The result is a main dining area of typically Scandinavian understated luxury, a sort of sumptuous minimalism. The white panels (actually made of MDF), create a subtly decorative backdrop – Lindvall says he wanted the design to act as a kind of discreet wallpaper to the dining, but also to suggest a contemporary interpretation of what the interior of an alpine hut could look like. These panels also allow for very gently diffused lighting in the room, which the designer compares to a 'modern igloo'.

Most of the fittings are bespoke, and those that aren't, such as the chairs (designed by Lindvall for Swedish manufacturer Skandiform and called Lui), are modified to fit the space; there is even a special double-sized version of the chair that can be discreetly wheeled out for the comfort of larger regulars. A simple cabinet made from Zebrano wood divides the two 'arms' of the space.

Next to the kitchen, which is visible through the large serving hatch, is the chef's table. The space is decorated with mosaic tiling and flower motifs, and is used for treating special guests to wine-tasting or trials of new dishes. A trip to the toilets repeats the unusual combination of austerity and luxury that is apparent in the rest of the restaurant.

4

5

4 A simple storage unit of zebrano wood breaks up the two arms of the main seating area of the restaurant.

5 The vivid mosaic walls of the tasting and private dining area provide a contrast with the studied minimalism of the main restaurant.

6　The walls feature white MDF
　panels with concealed lighting to
　create a 'modern igloo', while the
　seating is a modified version of
　the Lui chair that was previously
　designed by the architect for
　manufacturer Skandiform.

SWEETGREEN

Designers
**CORE**
Size
167 sq m (1798 sq ft)
Date
2009
Location
BETHESDA, MARYLAND,
USA

**BURGER BARS,
CAFETERIAS AND OTHER
SMALL RESTAURANTS**

'**WE CHASED THEM OUT** the office when they first came in,'
says Peter Hapstak of design group Core about his unlikely
prospective clients. 'They didn't have a business plan, just
two bits of paper. So we educated them and they came back
two weeks later with a serious proposal.'

And so a collaborative venture began, in which Core, a
large design consultancy specializing in restaurants, not
only designed the original and subsequent SweetGreen
restaurants, but mentored their young clients in the other
aspects of running a restaurant business.

Fresh from university, Nicolas Jammet, Nathaniel Ru and
Jonathan Neman had worked on a concept during their final
year for fast food that would be healthy and sustainable.
They envisaged a simple restaurant that would serve quick
and convenient meals, but that would have both health and
gourmet aspirations. It would also combine two separate and
relatively recent trends – a salad bar and frozen yogurt.

The three also had clear ideas about how the restaurant
should look. 'They wanted a high-impact design statement.
But compared to the competition, they also have a very
high commitment to it being green,' says project architect
Hapstak. The concept developed by Core was 'to almost

1

2

1 The quaint exterior of the original Sweetgreen in Georgetown, Washington, DC.

2 View from outside of the design for the new restaurant in Bethesda, Maryland.

wrap the restaurant in a leaf', which Hapstak sees as both symbolic and metaphorical. The enormous leaf wall graphics were then developed in collaboration with graphic designers Unison.

'Green isn't usually a good food colour but we think it really works here,' says Hapstak, adding that a lot of work was done to make the green leaves of the salad that are central to the SweetGreen offer really stand out on the wall behind the service area.

The original restaurant in Georgetown, Washington, DC, was a cute little house on an urban prairie. While highly profitable, the 46 sq m (495 sq ft) restaurant was just too small and the business was doing well enough to expand. So two new locations were selected by Greens Restaurant Group, including one in nearby Bethesda, Maryland. This allowed the designers to develop the design on a slightly larger canvas. While the Bethesda restaurant (and its new sister in Washington's Dupont Circle) is a lively space, Hapstak says it is also a very pragmatic and logical one, with careful consideration given to the flow through it.

SweetGreen's food is carefully selected for its sustainability – local organic produce is selected where possible, and red meat isn't sold. The salad containers are reusable, recycled paper and soy inks are used for bags and napkins, and canvas bags are available for takeaways. Like the food and packaging, the specification of the interior had to major on eco-credentials. Many of the materials are either reclaimed or recycled. Antique hickory, sourced from barns in nearby Virginia, was used for the walls and millwork, while the furniture is recycled out of bowling alley floors. This was sourced after one of the clients, Nicolas, chanced on the work of Jim Malone's company Counterevolution in Brooklyn. The flooring seems standard but is made of tiles with a large recycled content. Even the wall covering is made with eco-friendly biodegradable ink and adhesive. Simple energy-efficient fluorescent lighting strips hang at different heights from the ceiling, supplementing the light that comes in from the restaurant's open front.

3 The design concept was for a space to be 'wrapped' in a leaf to signal its green credentials. The furniture was created using recycled bowling alley floors.

189

## sweetgreen signature salads

**ese chicken**  $8

pped romaine, grilled chicken, shredded
ts, edamame, crispy wonton strips;
ed with a miso ginger dressing.

**rese**  $8

r spinach & mesclun with grape
otes, fresh mozzarella, fresh basil;
ed with a balsamic vinaigrette.

la wrap.

**guacamole greens**  $9
"guac deconstructed"

mesclun with grilled chicken or shrimp,
fresh avocado, grape tomatoes, red onion,
crushed tortilla chips; topped with a lime
cilantro jalapeno vinaigrette.

**chic p**  $8
[shĕk or sheek]

mesclun & baby spinach with grilled
chicken, chick peas, roasted peppers,
cucumbers, garlic pita chips; topped
with a lemon hummus tahini dressing.

**le parisien**  $9

baby arugula with roasted turkey, brie,
pears, toasted almonds; topped with a
champagne vinaigrette

**the bondi**  $9

mesclun & baby arugula with grilled
chicken, avocado, sweet corn, hearts
of palm, wasabi peas; topped with a
white balsamic vinaigrette.

**curry gold**  $8

chopped romaine with grilled
chicken, dried cranberries, coconut,
celery, toasted almonds; topped with
a curry pineapple yogurt dressing.

**all salads are served with warm bread**

**wrap-it-up**
any signature salad can be wrapped in a spinach tortilla wrap.

**santorini**  $9

chopped romaine with roasted sh
feta cheese, grapes, fresh mint, ch
splash of lemon juice; topped with
cucumber basil yogurt dressing.

**la scala**  $9

chopped romaine with sliced sala
fresh mozzarella, chickpeas, grape
tomatoes, fresh basil; topped with
red wine vinaigrette.

4

4 The designers strove to make the
trays of salad and free produce
stand out and seem as enticing
as possible.

5 Floor plan
1) Entrance
2) Dining
3) Food service
4) Office
5) Female toilet
6) Male toilet
7) Kitchen

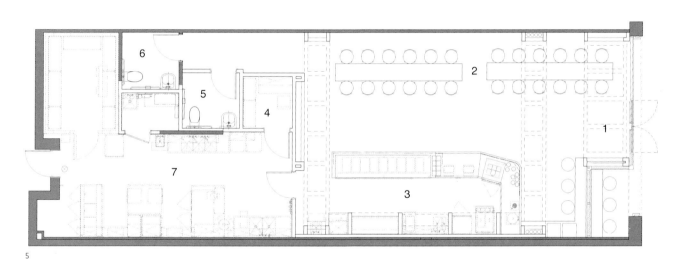

5

# 'WE WANTED TO ALMOST WRAP THE RESTAURANT IN A LEAF.'

## BOOLEAN (TOKYO UNIVERSITY TETSUMON CAFÉ)

Designers
**TORAFU ARCHITECTS**
Size
**48 sq m (517 sq ft)**
Date
**2007**
Location
**TOKYO, JAPAN**

**BURGER BARS, CAFETERIAS AND OTHER SMALL RESTAURANTS**

**LIKE SLICES FROM A** giant Swiss cheese, the walls and benches of this café have enormous holes cut out of them, creating unexpected vistas and openings. Originally, this area had simply been a blank open space to one side of the entrance to the Faculty of Medicine Experimental Research Building on the Hongo campus of the University of Tokyo. Torafu Architects, made up of Shinya Kamuro and Koichi Suzuno (who lectures at the University of Tokyo), were commissioned to create a design that would transform this space into a café.

Typical of institutional spaces, the designers say it was an empty, undefined area where a vending machine and hard surfaces predominated: marble floor and stone walls; stainless steel, and glass for the windows. Proving how effective a simple intervention can be, Torafu conceived a minimal and ingenious strategy to soften the space. Two large wooden panels, both L-shaped, would be erected: one that would function as a partition wall, the other as a bench for seating. As they wanted this to be a sociable space, they decided to cut large, seemingly random, circular shapes out of these panels.

'Imagining variously-sized spheres floating around in three-dimensional space, we cut circles out of the partition wall and bench as if the floating spheres burst and made holes on contact with them,' explain the designers. 'People can see the surrounding scenery through the holes on the partition wall and hang out with other people sitting on the bench. Holes overlapping each other make the place feel more open, as if there were floating spheres passing through the wall and ceiling, and framed scenery through the hole provides a new perspective from which customers can view everyday life.'

Another bench, with similar cut-outs, sits on the terrace in front of the café and faculty entrance.

1

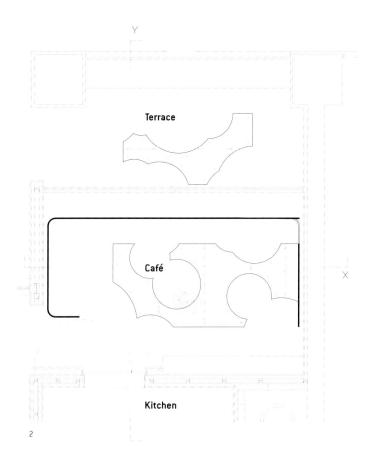

1 Simple bold wood panels with holes cut into them like Swiss cheese transform a bland foyer into a distinctive café.

2 Floor plan.

3 Section drawing.

Terrace

Café

Kitchen

2

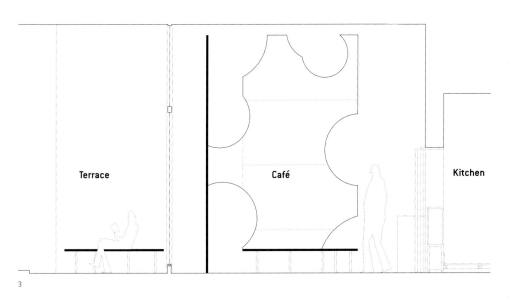

Terrace

Café

Kitchen

3

4 The playful geometry of the wooden walls curve through a right angle to form a casual seating area.

5 The holes cut into the wood panels frame visitors and create sightlines.

'WE CUT CIRCLES OUT OF THE PARTITION WALL AND BENCH, AS IF THE FLOATING SPHERES BURST AND MADE HOLES ON CONTACT WITH THEM.'

**FISH 349**

Designers
**TERROIR**
Size
**76.5 sq m (823 sq ft)**
main dining room
**59 sq m (635 sq ft)**
function room
Date
**2005/2007**
Location
**HOBART, TASMANIA,
AUSTRALIA**

**BURGER BARS,
CAFETERIAS AND OTHER
SMALL RESTAURANTS**

**SITUATED ON A LARGE** bay, Hobart is a city with a reputation for its food culture. Every year the city, capital of the island of Tasmania, hosts a waterfront food celebration called the Taste Festival. Hobart's coastal location also makes locally sourced seafood a popular choice all year round.

On a commercial strip of Elizabeth Street, a major road that runs through the centre of the city and its suburbs, lies Fish 349, a vibrant seafood restaurant. It's in a Georgian building with a 1970s extension, and the restaurant's large glass front engages openly with the street outside.

Local architects Terroir had designed the original restaurant in 2005, transforming the space that had once been a grocery into a lively and striking restaurant. The designers very much wanted to preserve its relation to the street outside with carefully considered sightlines and pathways. On entering the restaurant, you first find yourself in a clearly delineated and separate reception area, differentiated by its concrete floor, which also allows you to look into the open-plan kitchen. The main dining room to the right has a dark stained plywood floor and, on its far wall, a large busy graphic, whose graffiti-like quality counters the dark solemnity of the rest of the fittings. It's one of several

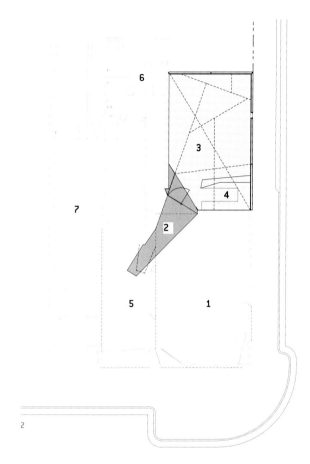

1 Fractured graphic decoration of the
  exterior of the restaurant and its
  extension hint at the design of the
  interior space.

2 Floor plan
  1) Existing restaurant
  2) Function room entry
  3) Function room
  4) Bar
  5) Kitchen
  6) Toilets
  7) Entrance lobby

2

instances where graphics, including – unusually – the exterior of the building, add dynamism and playfulness to the otherwise predictable architectural fabric that the designers inherited.

A small space to the rear of the building, which had served as a car park, provided expansion space when the owners of the restaurant decided to add a private function room to the restaurant two years later. Again, Terroir were commissioned, and the new space was quickly put together with precast concrete walls, allowing more attention and money to be spent on the interior and decoration.

As designers of the original space, the architects were sensitive to the needs of the existing as well as the new space. 'The opportunity to add a function room to this already "complete" space, immediately suggested a quality of "otherness" for the addition – a simple enlargement would have destroyed the identity of the existing dining room,' they explain.

Their idea, however, was an extreme development of elements of the previous work, particularly the graphics. The architects describe the concept as 'a fractured external container, struggling to contain the vibrancy of the interior space, with precise fragments giving way to form windows and skylights. The internal lining reinforces the fractured quality, taking further cues from the origami-like patterning of the restaurants' established logo.'

The 'shattered' space is constructed from lime-washed plywood panels, and visual intrigue is created by using dark areas to create false shadows or being arbitrarily cut away to become windows or skylights. And the dark restaurant floor is carried over from the main space into the function room and up part of the rear wall to further confuse immediate perceptions of the space.

Seating 45, the function room has its own bar and is almost as big as the main restaurant, but is intended for special social occasions or business functions. The restaurant has a menu restricted to seafood and chips, along with salads and ice cream desserts. As well as locally caught produce, it also serves Tasmanian wines and beers.

3 The restaurant is housed in a Georgian building with a 1970s extension on one of Hobart's main thoroughfares.

'A FRACTURED EXTERNAL CONTAINER, STRUGGLING TO CONTAIN THE VIBRANCY OF THE INTERIOR SPACE, WITH PRECISE FRAGMENTS GIVING WAY TO FORM WINDOWS AND SKYLIGHTS.'

3

4

4 The fractured graphics of the function room play visual games, such as a floor that seems to continue up the rear wall.

5 The function room also contains its own bar.

5

6 Entrance to the function room showing the relation of its fractured visuals to the design of the main restaurant.

7 View into the main restaurant from the entrance lobby showing the graffiti-like graphic on a side wall.

6

EXIT

7

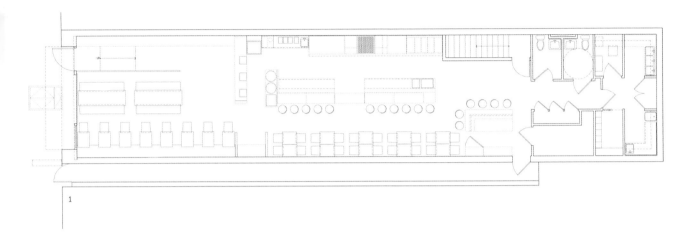

1

Designers
ROCKWELL GROUP
Size
185 sq m (1991 sq ft)
Date
2006
Location
NEW YORK, USA

**BRGR**

**BURGER BARS, CAFETERIAS AND OTHER SMALL RESTAURANTS**

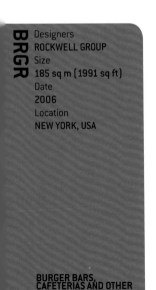

**BRGR IS THE BRAINCHILD** of New York restaurateur Chris Russell who, with a variety of successful concepts under his belt, wanted to reinterpret the much-maligned hamburger for a more fashion- and health-conscious Chelsea clientele.

The food itself was the starting point, and Russell spent a year researching ingredients and combinations for brgr's menu, which includes vegetarian offerings and unusual toppings such as Roquefort and horseradish, as well as the classics. Rockwell Group was commissioned to design the interior, and – given the central role of the food – it developed a design based around 'the craft of the burger'.

This was expressed by making the kitchen centre stage in the restaurant, and its gleaming high-tech appliances are a dominant decorative feature, especially the 4.3 m (14 ft) high stainless steel extractor hood. The open plan allows diners to see the ingredients being prepared and cooked right in the heart of the space. Ingredients are stored in wire racks suspended above the heads of diners eating in the front part of the restaurant, while slate blackboards are hung with information about the food scribbled in chalk.

Customers arriving at the restaurant pick up a menu at the entrance and order at the counter, before sitting down either at the tables or the bar in front of the kitchen to eat. As with the food, classic American fast food design is given an updating tweak. There's a combination of traditional elements, such as exposed brick wall, and new, more luxurious elements, such as the oversized tiles on the counter embossed with the restaurant's logo, which was also designed by Rockwell Group.

The translucent orange acrylic of the Italian metal framed seats is picked up by pink tube lighting, and a banquette made up of small, 20 cm diameter (8 in), cushions in different bright colours runs down the wall of one side of the restaurant. Bespoke bar stools and tables were designed by Rockwell Group but inspired by vintage diner designs, and the tables themselves are covered in butcher's paper during opening hours.

The restaurant occupies a double-height space in a turn-of-the-century building, but only the bottom storey is occupied, with the beams dividing the floors left open to add a sense of drama to the space.

2 The restaurant occupies the bottom half of a double-height space in New York's hip Chelsea neighbourhood.

3

'THE KITCHEN WAS MADE CENTRE STAGE OF THE RESTAURANT.'

4

3 Bespoke bar stools and oversized white tiles were selected by the designers, as were orange Italian acrylic chairs.

4 Pink tube lighting accentuates the longitudinal feel of the space.

5&6 The stainless steel hi tech kitchen appliances and extractor were left exposed to work as an integral decorative element.

5

6

7 A banquette with small colourful cushions runs down one side of the restaurant.

**PROEF**

Designer
MARIJE VOGELZANG
Size
FLEXIBLE
Date
2006
Location
AMSTERDAM,
NETHERLANDS

**BURGER BARS,
CAFETERIAS AND OTHER
SMALL RESTAURANTS**

1 Overhead view of the central table in Marije Vogelzang's studio, which is transformed to host a variety of 'eating events'.

2

# 'THE DINING EXPERIENCE IS MORE A DESIGNED RITUAL THAN A MEAL IN A RESTAURANT.'

**AMSTERDAM-BASED MARIJE VOGELZANG** typifies the very
conceptual approach of contemporary Dutch design. Rather
than designing objects or spaces, her work revolves around
food, or what she terms 'eating design', something distinct
from food design or restaurant design. The customs, social
interactions and methodologies of consuming food are taken
apart or surreally reassembled in her various projects, which
include meals hosted in her Amsterdam studio.

The studio is transformed into a temporary 45-seat
informal restaurant, Proef Amsterdam (*proef* means 'to taste'
in Dutch]. Its format is always open to reinterpretation but
is usually structured around the central table. The clients
can vary from a large multinational company to the radical
design group Droog, and, while food is served, it is the social
experience and interaction that is the primary focus. 'My
starting point, my way of working is different from a caterer,
because I aim for a kind of story that I want to tell,' Vogelzang
explains. 'The environment has an important influence that
is not always conscious – but I do think a space can make
you feel comfortable or not. The acoustics, the materials, the
climate, and, yes, even the taste of the interior designer, all
have an influence on the experience of the people.'

3 The Connection Dinner, devised for furniture company Droog for a Christmas event in 2006, featuring a table cloth of dough superimposed on a set table.

3

Just outside the studio is a herb garden and an area where chickens lay their eggs. Inside, cooks work in the studio, transforming Proef Amsterdam into a communal space. The dining experience itself is more a designed ritual than a meal in a restaurant or a dinner party. The presentation of the food is unconventional and designed to provoke different emotional responses in the diners. For instance, food can be served on broken plates, or loaves of bread might be re-engineered as food receptacles. On one occasion, the tablecloth was reversed so that the diners were required to poke their heads through holes in order to get at their food; on another occasion anglepoise lamps were used to heat the dessert.

Proef Amsterdam had a predecessor – Proef Rotterdam. This was a more conventional café that Vogelzang established a couple of years earlier, when she was fresh out of the Design Academy Eindhoven. 'I had lots of interesting ideas and wanted to put them into practice. Suddenly you realize that reality is very different to what you would – as a designer – consider reality to be. It was a great learning experience for me to realize, after falling on my face a few times, that sometimes some really silly things can stop you from achieving your goal.' In 2009 Proef Rotterdam was closed and sold, and has since re-opened as a more traditional café, now called Picknick, with Vogelzang retained as a consultant.

4 Diners stick their head through an
upturned table cloth to reach the
food at a Proef Amsterdam eating
event in 2006.

4

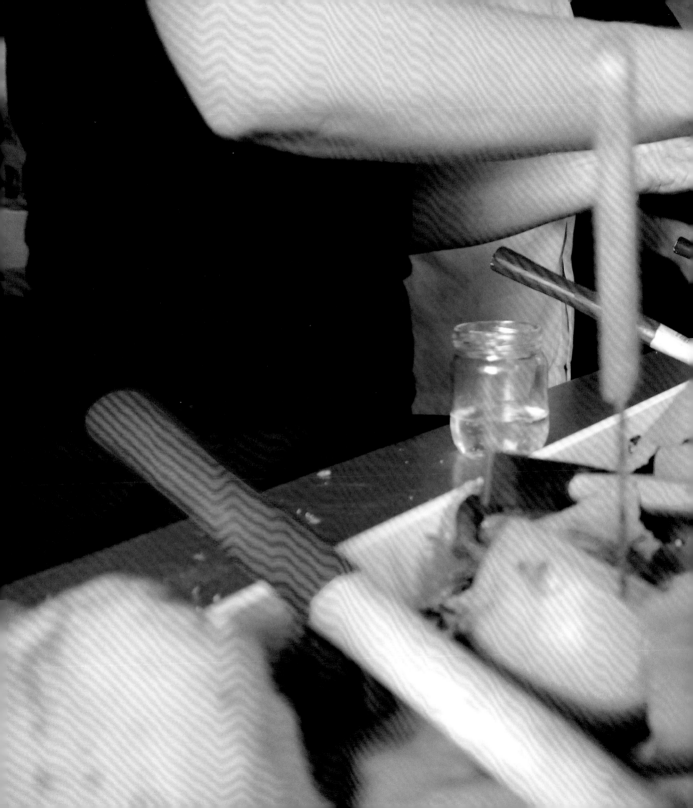

5 Diners are encouraged to use hammers rather than the more customary eating utensils in this eating design.

BLOSSOM

Designer
RYUJI NAKAMURA
Size
30 sq m (323 sq ft)
Date
2009
Location
NAGANO, JAPAN

BURGER BARS,
CAFETERIAS AND OTHER
SMALL RESTAURANTS

1 Two simple bentwood chairs punctuate the ethereal environment of this function room in Nagano, Japan.

2 The slight protrusion of the metal flowers creates a highly subtle decorative effect where different planes meet.

# 'I WANTED TO MAKE A PLACE WHERE PEOPLE COULD EAT SLOWLY.'

2

**TWELVE THOUSAND FLOWERS ADORN** a tiny private dining room, creating a special space for the unhurried appreciation of food. Blossom is part of Les Halles de Saison Sage, a restaurant in the historic city of Matsumoto in central Japan, which approached Tokyo-based designer Ryuji Nakamura to create a design that would make better use of this small adjoining space.

As it was very recently constructed, Nakamura says that the restaurant – and this simple room in particular – were very 'clean', making the brief of creating a 'better' space a challenge as there was no straightforward design problem to solve.

On consideration, he decided there was one element that could be improved – the mood of the person dining in the space – and that this could be achieved by means of decoration. 'I wanted to make a place where people could eat slowly,' explains Nakamura. 'A place where the guest doesn't get tired no matter what state he arrives in, and that wouldn't grate however long he was there.'

Opening the windows onto an external vista was not possible due to the erection of other buildings very close by, so an internal view had to be created, one that, moreover, could only have minimal reliance on window light.

Nakamura's solution, a subtle and unusual wallpaper made from 12,000 little metal flowers, creates an ethereal environment that is every bit as conducive to calm contemplation as traditional Zen architecture, but achieved by very different means.

The flowers are made of steel of a particular thickness, chosen for the warp that naturally results when it is laser cut, lending the individual cut petals their distinctive and subtle curve. Once cut, the petals were painted white and stuck to the walls, and with the protruding element, they cast a small shadow. Their distribution is random except where they meet intersecting walls so as to delicately etch the folds that define the space. The simple table and traditional central European bentwood chairs become almost like surreal props within the room.

3 Some 12,000 metal flowers were laser cut from metal in a controlled fashion to create a uniform warp.

Kara's Cupcakes

CONFECTIONERY RESTAURANTS

Designers
WONDERWALL
Graphics
GROOVISIONS
Art Direction
KOICHI ANDO, ANDO.
GALLERY.
Size
69.3 sq m (745.9 sq ft)
Date
2004
Location
TOKYO, JAPAN

CONFECTIONERY
RESTAURANTS

1 Shown here lit up at night, the 100%ChocolateCafé is a jewel-like presence on the ground floor of confectionery company Meiji's head office in Tokyo.

2 groovisions, a Tokyo graphic design consultancy, devised the colourful packaging scheme for the chocolate bars, where each flavour is readily identifiable from its number.

2

**TOKYO'S CONSUMERS ARE NOTORIOUSLY** design-aware and discerning, expecting novelty and quality in equal measure. Meiji, a well established and very popular confectionery brand, conceived the novel idea of a chocolate café that would function as an outlet for a premium line of chocolates but that would also allow the chocolates to be eaten on-site in a café. It's a concept that has proved popular and has been frequently imitated since.

100%ChocolateCafé is located on the ground floor of Meiji's office building in the commercial district of Kyobashi in Tokyo, a few blocks away from the prime shopping area of Ginza. An all-star cast of designers was assembled to develop the concept, brand, space and packaging, all overseen and art directed by Koichi Ando. The resulting new brand, 100%ChocolateCafé, makes no explicit reference to its parent, Meiji, and its mass-market chocolate products.

Katayama Masamichi, the cult Japanese designer of firm Wonderwall, describes his concept for the café's interior as a 'chef's table in the kitchen'; a space in which people are given the impression of being invited to a sampling of delights. In common with his other retail and leisure designs, 100%ChocolateCafé presents an unusual environment aimed

3

4

3  Packets of colourfully packaged
   chocolate are presented in an open
   display case, as if they were tile
   samples or books.

4  Shimmering chilled glass cabinets
   present the chocolates as though
   they are precious wares.

5  The ceiling features a panel
   that seems to be a giant slab
   of chocolate.

at delivering a total experience of the brand. The theme of chocolate inspires each small detail of the interior, which still manages to appear as classy and luxurious rather than contrived or gimmicky. The suspended ceiling is the space's most dramatic feature – it seems like a giant, upside-down slab of chocolate. Mosaic tiling on the walls and floor pick up on the milk-chocolate tiling theme, while the counter and furniture are also of a rich, chocolate brown. On the wall opposite the counter, there is a bank of chilled glass showcases for the blocks of chocolate, subtly lit to create a wonderful glowing effect.

The brand's concept allows for one flavour for every day of the year, and customers can also buy exquisitely packaged gift boxes of either the full 365 varieties, or a slightly slimmed down set of 56 pre-selected varieties. The chocolates are grouped by a variety of criteria. This can be by flavour, varying from the classics to more unusual flavours, such as cheese and milk tea; by the country of the origins of the cacao beans used; or according to the different kinds of sweeteners used, such as wasabon or sugar.

Each of the different flavours is identified by a large number on striking packaging designed by Tokyo-based graphic design consultancy groovisions. Their presentation, in graded strong colours, provides a visual contrast to the luxurious warm hues of the interior design and furniture. Their presentation in racks evokes that of tile samples or library books.

As well as serving as an outlet for these premium chocolates (and various associated merchandise), it is also a genuine chocolate café offering ingenious chocolate-related confectionery and dishes served with the tea and coffee, such as croissants accompanied with different flavoured chocolate dippers. The continuing success of the café prompted a temporary installation in the Isetan Department Store in Shinjuku in Japan in 2007 as part of an international chocolate celebration.

5

'THE SUSPENDED CEILING SEEMS LIKE A GIANT, UPSIDE-DOWN SLAB OF CHOCOLATE.'

Designers
MONTALBA ARCHITECTS,
INC
Size
72 sq m (775 sq ft)
Date
2006
Location
SAN FRANCISCO, USA

KARA'S CUPCAKES

CONFECTIONERY
RESTAURANTS

3249

Kara's Cupcakes

1

1 A minimal window display of
  individual cup cakes is a cute
  divergence from the usual practice
  of filling the front with cakes.

2&3 Plan and section
   1) Entrance
   2) Window display
   3) Display case
   4) Point of sale
   5) Eating counter
   6) Preparation area

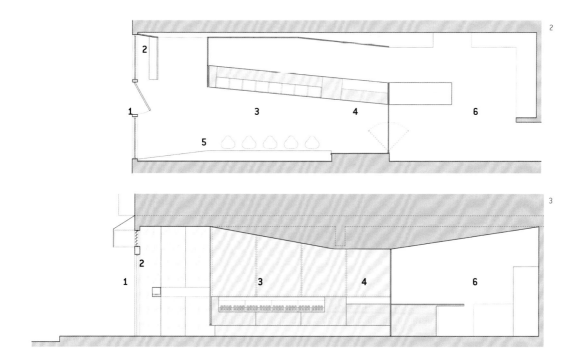

# 'THE MAIN COUNTER HOUSING THE CUPCAKES COULDN'T BE SEEN DIRECTLY FROM OUTSIDE.'

**FOUNDED BY THE SWEET-**toothed daughter of a dentist, Kara's Cupcakes sells its diminutive cakes in a space that is as carefully crafted as its wares. What started as a home bakery business rapidly became successful enough to warrant its own store. And by the time Montalba Architects were approached to design its first store, Michael Lind of Montalba Architects already had Jon Ritt, then at Pool, onboard as branding consultant and had earmarked a site in San Francisco.

Located in the Marina district, this was a rather dark space that had once been a yoga studio. 'The challenge for us was how to bring light into the space and sculpt the visual experience,' remembers David Montalba. As there was a lot going on visually in the street, Montalba sought to create space for the store by keeping things quiet rather than shouting loudly. 'Like music, it's about the space between the tones,' he says.

The resulting design has a restrained and pared-down window display presenting individual tiny cupcakes in a way that wittily subverts the pastry-shop convention of showing as many of your wares as possible. Inside, the main counter housing the cupcakes was placed parallel to the view, so it

225

4

couldn't be seen directly from outside – to fully appreciate the display the passerby has to enter the store.

The counter has trays for the different sorts of cupcakes, which vary from the classic 'Sweet Vanilla' to a more exotic chocolate cupcake with a creamy smooth peanut butter and milk chocolate ganache frosting. Parallel to the main display is a wall-mounted table that runs down the wall along with an area of seating to allow the cakes to be consumed on the premises.

To keep the space from feeling dark and dingy, an unusual wave-like ceiling was constructed to 'pull' light through the tight space. Additional spotlighting echoes the shapes of the cupcakes.

The other main challenge, says Montalba, was to articulate the public area and private preparation areas of the space in as sensitive a fashion as possible. This was achieved with panels of speciality glass laminated with a pink inner layer to create a subtle translucent effect. As well as dividing the space, these panels provide colour and also carry some of the explanatory graphics for customers.

Teak panelling is used for the rest of the space and counter. Given the subject matter it would have been easy to go for a less restrained approach, with something more gimmicky and playful, but this was deliberately avoided. 'We like to think we don't design kitsch things,' says Montalba. 'It's not always about creating a single idea that happens all at once. The merchandise contrasts with but also complements the design.'

Four other stores followed; another in San Francisco as well as in Napa, Palo Alto and San Jose.

5 Translucent pink glass panels
containing customer information
contrast with the teak used for the
counter and panelling.

5

6 Only once inside Kara's Cupcakes do visitors get to see the cupcakes in all their variety.

Designers
LENS°ASS ARCHITECTEN
Size
75 sq m (807 sq ft)
Date
2009
Location
LONDON, UK

CONFECTIONERY
RESTAURANTS

1

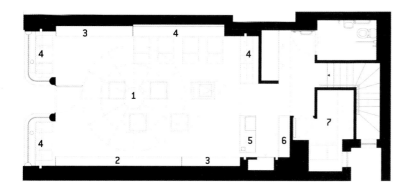

2

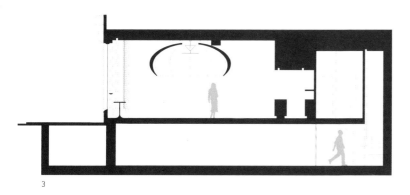

3

**KNOWN AS HIGH PRIESTS** of chocolate, Artisan du Chocolat is a UK company that sells freshly prepared chocolates with unusual flavours such as tobacco or lemon verbena. Lauded by food critics, it also hosts popular chocolate tasting events. To build on this enthusiastic foodie following, Artisan du Chocolat decided to go one step further and add a dedicated chocolateria to its existing London stores, approaching iconoclastic Belgian designer Bart Lens to design the space.

A novel element was added to the nascent concept of the chocolateria – a well-known mixologist was enlisted to devise a series of chocolate cocktails that could be consumed on the premises along with other chocolate delicacies. The idea was to make the tasting and eating of chocolate a more sociable and relaxed experience.

The resulting design is typical of Bart Lens' work: a bit strange and unsettling; it aims to get people asking questions. While it is far from an unfriendly space, the designer wasn't too concerned about making the space instantly decipherable – at first glance it could just as easily come across as a perfume shop or hair salon as a chocolateria.

The café is dominated by an impossibly large, bulbous

## 'AN IMPOSSIBLY LARGE, BULBOUS LAMP CREATES THE EFFECT OF A ROOM WITHIN A ROOM.'

4  The interior of the gigantic °XXXL
features images of a cocoa
plantation while other elements
of the design allude to the various
stages of chocolate production.

5

5 Sophisticated, silent refrigeration
  units are concealed within the
  glass chocolate display cabinets.

6 Detail of the panoramic cocoa
  plantation graphic on the inside of
  the lamp, applied on a film using
  an automotive technology.

7 The chocolate slab-themed tables
  were suggested by the client.

lamp. It creates the effect of a room within a room, whose extent is somewhat mysterious. The lamp itself is a development of the ºXXXL lamp that Bart Lens had earlier presented at the Milan Furniture Fair, and it only just fits into the space. Inside the lamp there's a jungle of green that contrasts with the highly controlled finish of the rest of the shop. Assembled in 12 sections, the lamp's plastic, double-shelled construction is largely held together by gravity apart from a dab of bonding at the top. Printing the panoramic image of a cocoa plantation inside the lamp proved to be a technical challenge, and the designers ended up using a specialist film material often used for decorating the bodywork of cars. The idea of showing the plantation was to create an intriguing environment, and to communicate the source of the beans and processes behind the confectionery on offer.

During the process, there was a fairly relaxed collaboration between designer and client; the client suggested the chocolate-themed tables. (The rich brown paint of the exterior is likewise a reference to chocolate.) The cylindrical stools were adapted and shortened versions of another earlier design by Lens – the º2chevaux, inspired by a gymnasium vaulting horse.

The seating is seamlessly integrated with the displays of chocolate for sale. Given chocolate's tendency to melt (and the lack of preservatives in Artisan du Chocolat's delicatessen confectionery), cooling was perhaps the designers' biggest challenge, beside the oversized lamp. Avoiding the conventional presentation of chocolates behind counters, the long open shelves contain highly sophisticated and silent cooling technology. The integrated lighting also had to be carefully considered so as not to create heat that would cause the chocolates to melt or perish.

The designers concurrently worked on a concession for Artisan du Chocolat in London department store Selfridges that would use many of the same elements.

6

7

Designer
MARTÍ GUIXÉ
Size
25 sq m (269 sq ft)
Date
2007
Location
TOKYO, JAPAN

CONFECTIONERY
RESTAURANTS

**THE IDEA OF A** concept restaurant is nothing new – a restaurant adopts a theme or outfit, like fancy dress on top of its usual everyday business dress. The Candy Restaurant, open for a mere five days in 2007, is the very opposite. It is a concept that pretends to be a restaurant, and the paraphernalia of a restaurant is its 'outfit' or its physical expression.

Food has long been an obsession for Catalan designer Martí Guixé, who has produced many books and exhibitions on the subject. He stands back and interprets 'food design' in a different way, removing it from its usual baggage. 'Food design makes it possible to think of food as an edible designed product, an object that negates any reference to cooking, tradition and gastronomy,' he writes.

In the Candy Restaurant, as the name suggests, the food served was a variety of sweets. Confectionery is normally eaten informally with only the minimum of social ceremony, as a sort of private pleasure, but here its consumption is structured and socialized. Visiting the 'restaurant', the visitor would make his or her choice from a menu, which presented formulations of confectionery as though they were usual restaurant fare. This would then be carefully prepared by a

1

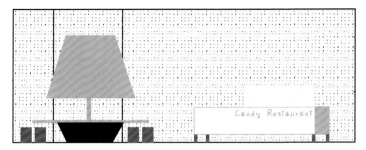

1 Candy Restaurant graphics and colour palette that is reminiscent of chocolate, with a touch of luxurious gold.

2 Interior concept showing the low table, which seats 17, with huge gold lamp, glass work area and candy wallpaper.

# Candy Restaurant

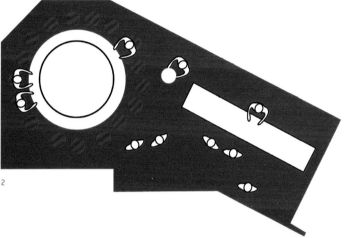

2

'candy chef' on little trays with handwritten comments about what was being presented, and then served. Visitors would sit at a large circular central table under the light of a giant lamp. Guixé writes that this 'formalizes the occasional act of eating a candy by bringing it into the rituals of everyday food, and transforming this everyday into a more contemporary experience and feeling.'

You might be forgiven for thinking that the exquisitely crafted trays of bento takeaway food for which Japan is famous were an inspiration, but Guixé says this was not the case: 'No, bento is just takeaway food. The Candy Restaurant came from a commission from a communication agency to do a project in cross media, to reinforce the campaign for Marui, which was done with the slogan "fashion therapy" showing in the printed media images of pills, I thought to extend the image of pills in candies was very coherent, and I proposed a Candy Restaurant, a place where you eat candies.'

It is an engagement with the process of consumption, but not a critical one. The whole experience of a visit to the Candy Restaurant is meant to be delightful, from the sweet taste of the confectionery to the delightful naïve logo and graphics. It is intended to encourage consumption and engage with it as a conscious act of fashion.'

The Candy Restaurant was located on the first floor of the enormous Marunouchi complex by Tokyo Station, close to the prime retail area of Ginza, and was commissioned by Japanese women's fashion company Marui.

3

3 Chef's work area with glass display cases.

4 Candy chef meticulously creating a customer order, which would be presented with the chef's handwritten comments.

5 The light-hearted concept sketch by Martí Guixé for Candy including all the accoutrements of a 'restaurant', from menus and chefs, to the actual design of the serving trays and the candy-inspired wallpaper.

4

# 'THE RESTAURANT FORMALIZES THE OCCASIONAL ACT OF EATING A CANDY BY BRINGING IT INTO THE RITUALS OF EVERYDAY FOOD.'

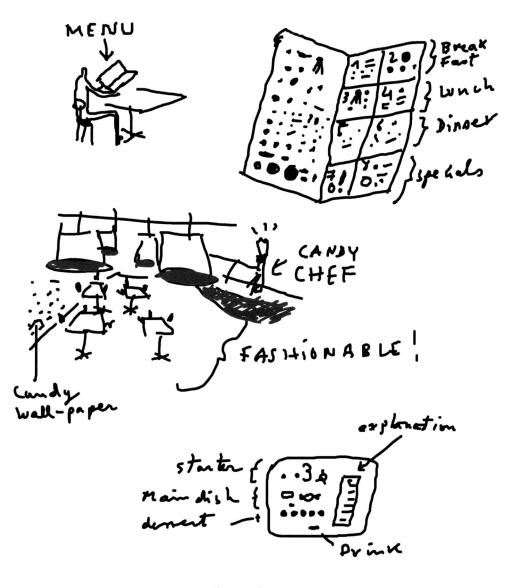

CANDY-RESTAURANT

6  The space is dominated by the huge gold lamp overhanging the dining table, and has a backdrop of candy motif wallpaper.

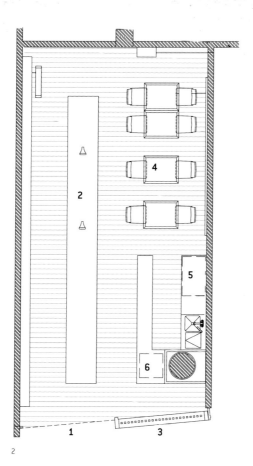

1 The front was intended to pique
the curiosity of passersby, with
the shelves of tiny digital numbers
more akin to a conceptual art work
than shop or café.

2 Floor plan
1) Entrance
2) Central display table
3) Window display
4) Seating area
5) Drink and food preparation area
6) Counter and till

2

**IN A FAIRLY ORDINARY** mall full of fairly ordinary shops, the stroller happens upon a curious shop window, full of numbers. 'We wanted it to look like an art installation,' says Chris Lee, creative director of Asylum, who created this outlet for the specialist Singaporean retailer Chocolate Research Facility.

'We wanted people to go "Oh wow, what's that?" and be curious enough to go inside to find out what is being sold,' he says. Once inside, the visitor discovers a chocolate emporium. In addition to the exquisitely packaged chocolate available to take away, laid out in tidy piles like paperbacks in a bookshop, to the right there is a small café serving chocolate-related fare such as hot chocolate and brownies.

If the brand was Asylum's starting point for the design of Frolick (see page 124), then the point of departure for the Chocolate Research Facility was the packaging, and a concept was evolved that would position it centre stage. One hundred different flavours are offered, from green apple with dried pear to lychee martini or red bean milk chocolate, and each of the different series of chocolates (such as the nuts series, or alcohol series) has its own design identity. The packaging itself has two stages – a monochrome outer box, which sets the scene for the vibrant colour of the actual packaging of the bar itself. The chocolate is stored in little boxes on a wall on the left-hand side of the shop – suggested, Lee says, by the storage systems of traditional Asian pharmacies.

In keeping with this slightly medicinal/medical theme, hinted at in any case by its playful name, a large mirror sits on the opposite wall. This is intended to suggest the two-way mirror of a research lab, hiding imaginary white-coated researchers investigating your chocoholism. A stained pine floor was chosen to soften the overall effect – adding a touch of warmth, it prevents the space from feeling too clinical.

The Chocolate Research Facility defines itself as 'concept boutique-cum-café'. Its website (also designed by Asylum) features a wall of melting chocolate that gradually drips down the page, evoking the rear wall of the café itself, which has a similar feature. A subsequent Chocolate Research Facility in Shanghai was also designed by Asylum, but following a different concept.

3.

**'WE WANTED PEOPLE TO GO "OH WOW, WHAT'S THAT?"'**

4

3 Some of the chocolates are laid out in tidy stacks on a central display table while others are in a wall of pull-out cardboard drawers that are suggestive of a traditional Asian pharmacy.

4 Central to the tongue-in-cheek 'scientific' concept is the idea of the laboratory, here hinted at by a mirror that pretended to be one way glass shielding customers from white-coated scientists at the other side studying the phenomenon of chocolate.

5 The effect of melting chocolate dripping down the walls is repeated in animated form on Chocolate Research Facility's website. The chocolate theme is picked up by the tables, but the moulded white plastic chairs are a classic design by Charles and Ray Eames.

5

6, 7&8 Each group of chocolate
flavours and types has its own
packaging identity, varying from a
simple black and white approach,
through to a pixilated design
and another featuring two-tone
sampling of retro typography.

6

7

# PROJECT CREDITS

## 100% CHOCOLATE CAFÉ

1F Meiji Seika head-office building
2-4-16 Kyobashi
Chuoku
Tokyo
Japan
www.choco-cafe.jp
**Design** Wonderwall
www.wonder-wall.com
**Graphics** groovisions
www.groovisions.com
**Creative direction** Ando Gallery
www.andogallery.co.jp

## ARTISAN DU CHOCOLAT

Westbourne Grove
London W2 4UL
UK
www.artisanduchocolat.com
**Design** Lens°Ass Architecten
– Bart Lens and Andri Haflidason
www.lensass.be/
**Shopfitters** Newman Scott
**Cooling** Arco NV

## BLOOM IN THE PARK

Pildammsvägen 17
214 66 Malmö
Sweden
www.bloominthepark.se
**Design** Jonas Lindvall and Mikael Ling, Lindvall A & D
www.jonaslindvall.com
**Lighting** Ljus i Hus AB

## BLOSSOM

2F Les halles de saison sage
Takamiyahigashi, 1–28
Matsumoto-shi
Nagano
Japan
**Design** Ryuji Nakamura
www.ryujinakamura.com
**Construction** AD Design

## BOOLEAN (TOKYO UNIVERSITY TETSUMON CAFÉ)

7-3-1 Hongo
Bunkyo-ku
Tokyo 113-8654
Japan
**Design** Torafu Architects
www.torafu.com
**Lighting design** Maxray
**Construction** Inoue Industries

## BRGR

West 27th Street at 7th Avenue
New York, NY 10001
USA
www.brgr.us
**Design** Rockwell Group
www.rockwellgroup.com

## CAMPER FOODBALL

Closed – formerly at
Carrer d'Elisabets 9
El Raval
08001 Barcelona
Spain
www.camper.es
**Design** Martí Guixé
www.guixe.com

## CANDY RESTAURANT

Temporary event at Café Ease
1F Marunouchi Building
Tokyo
Japan
**Concept/Art director** Martí Guixé
**Creative director** Morihiro Harano
**Executive producer** Osamu Enari
**Food coordinator** Kyoko Hirosawa
**Copywriter** Hidetoshi Kuranari
**Designer** Yusuke Kitani
**Producers** Ryuji Ueno, Koji Fujioka – Agency Drill Inc./ Dentsu Inc.
**Production** Hoseisha Co., Ltd/ Partners Inc.
**Client** Yurakucho Marui

## LA CASA AZUL VINOS AND ROOMS

Calle Palafox, 7
46001 Valencia
Spain
www.lacasaazulvinosandrooms.com
**Design** Herme Ciscar and Mónica García
www.hermeymonica.com
**Contractor** Montaje y Diseño de Oficina

## CHA CHA MOON

Closed – formerly at Whiteleys
Queensway
London W2 4YN
UK
**Architect** Kengo Kuma & Associates (Kengo Kuma, Ryukichi Tatsuki, Tomoyuki Hasegawa), Jane McKay Architects Limited (Jane McKay)
www.kkaa.co.jp
**Structural engineer** Michael Hadi Associates Ltd (Mike Hadi)
**M&E engineer** EEP (Nigel Bowater)
**Lighting designer** Firefly Lighting Design (John Lau)
**Project manager** Mark Alford & Co (Mark Alford)
**Contractor** Goodman Hichens (Nick Gardner)
**Electric installer** MCE Ltd (Martin Holmes)
**Mechanical installer** Sidney Cubbage (Dave Smith)

## CHOCOLATE RESEARCH FACILITY

9 Raffles Boulevard
01–30 Millenia Walk
Singapore 039596
www.chocolateresearchfacility.com
**Design** Asylum
www.theasylum.com.sg

## COSO CAFÉ

Piazza Sant'Onofrio, 14
90134 Palermo
Italy
**Architects** Francesco Moncada, Massimo Tepedino
**Interior designer** Ornella Gasbarro
**Client** Novelli s.r.l.

## THE DEPTFORD PROJECT

121–123 Deptford High Street
London SE8 4NS
UK
www.thedeptfordproject.com
**Design** Morag Myerscough,
Studio Myerscough
www.studiomyerscough.com
and Luke Morgan

## EAST BEACH CAFÉ

The Promenade
Sea Road
Littlehampton
West Sussex BN17 5GB
UK
www.eastbeachcafe.co.uk
**Design** Heatherwick Studio
www.heatherwick.com
**Lighting** Janet Turner and Into
Lighting
**Kitchen design** Alan Clayton
Design
**Structural engineer** Adams
Kara Taylor
**Steelwork** Littlehampton
Welding
**Contractor** Langridge
Developments

## ESPRESSO *K

Destroyed following fire
– formerly at the Delft
University of Technology
**Design** 2012 Architecten
www.2012architecten.nl

## ESTADO PURO

Plaza Canovas Del Castillo, 4
28014 Madrid
Spain
www.tapasenestadopuro.com
**Design** James & Mau
Architecture
www.jamesandmau.com
**Graphics** in collaboration with
Agency Full Mix
**Doorway** to hotel designed
by NI

## FISH 349

349 Elizabeth Street
North Hobart, 7000
Tasmania
Australia
www.fish349.com.au
**Design** Terroir Pty. Ltd.
**Design architect** Scott
Balmforth, Gerard Reinmuth,
Richard Blythe
**Other project team members**
Paul Sayers, Justin Hanlon,
Matthew Skirving, Alex Reed
www.terroir.com.au
**Contractor** Tascon Pty. Ltd.

## FROLICK

4 Kensington Park Road
Serangoon Gardens
Singapore 557256
www.frolick.com.sg
**Design** Asylum
www.theasylum.com.sg

## ILLY PUSH BUTTON CAFÉ

Temporary structure at the
2007 Venice Biennale
**Design** Adam Kalkin
www.architectureandhygiene.
com

## ITSU

1 Hanover Square
London W1S 1HA
UK
www.itsu.com
**Design** Afroditi Krassa
www.afroditi.com

## JOHN STREET TEA AND WINE

Langton House Hotel
67 John Street
Kilkenny
Ireland
www.langtons.ie
**Design** David Collins and
Simon Rawlings, Creative
Director –
David Collins Studio
www.davidcollins.com

## JULIA'S PASTA

Stationsplein 15
Central Station
Amsterdam
The Netherlands
**Interior Design** Merkx+Girod
architects
www.merkx-girod.com
**Project team** Evelyne Merkx,
Det van Oers, Sanne Oomen,
Klaas Cammelbeeck,
Raymond Leentvaar, Marlies
Hoevers, Ruben Bus
**Illustrations** Agata
Zwierzynska
**Graphic design** Irma Boom
**Contractor** van 't Wout, Alphen
a/d Rijn

## KARA'S CUPCAKES

3249 Scott Street
San Francisco, CA 94123
USA
www.karascupcakes.com
**Architect** Montalba Architects,
Inc.
**Branding consultant** POOL SF
**Consulting interior designer**
Think Pure
**Consulting lighting designer**
John Brubaker Architectural
Lighting Consultants
**Consulting general contractor**
NorCal Construction
Management Services LLC

## KIRSCHGARTEN CAFETERIA

Gymnasium Kirschgarten
Hermann Kinkelin-Str. 10
4051 Basel
Switzerland
gkg.edubs.ch
**Design** HHF architects
www.hhf.ch
**Client** Kanton Basel-Stadt
**Colour concept** Gido
Wiederkehr

## LITTLE CHEF

Popham Services
Micheldever
Winchester SO21 3SP
UK
www.little-chef.co.uk
**Design** Ab Rogers Design
**Graphics** Praline
**Interaction design** Dominic
Robson – Robson & Jones
**Contractors** ATLAS
**Furniture manufacturer** Ethos
Design Limited
**Lighting
manufacturer** Liminaires
Limited (Consultant)
**Floor** Ceramic tiles and glass
mosaic tiles: Domus Tiles;
vinyl floor: Altro
**Ceramic tile wall** Domus Tiles

## MCDONALD'S

www.mcdonalds.com
**Design** Philippe Avanzi, Atelier
Archange

## PIZZA BAR

Closed – was at
48 Ninth Avenue,
New York, NY 10011
USA
**Design** Ali Tayar, Parallel
Design
www.alitayar.com
**Graphics** Giovanni Russo

## PIZZA PEREZ

Via Costanza Bruno, 58
96100 Syracuse, Italy
www.pizzaperez.com
**Architect** Francesco Moncada
www.francescomoncada.com
**Graphics** Point Supreme,
Konstantinos Pantazis and
Marianna Rentzou

## THE PLANT CAFÉ ORGANIC

3352 Steiner Street
San Francisco, CA 94123
USA
www.theplantcafe.com
**Owner** Mark Lewis, Matthew
Guelke
**Architectural and interiors
team** Design Principal: Cass
Smith, Project Architect: Sean
Kennedy
**Designers** Scott Baltimore
and Laura Mans
**Lighting** Revolver Design,
Emeryville, CA
**Food service** Larry Ballinger,
Santa Rosa, CA
**Table tops** Lawrence Gandsey,
San Francisco, CA
**Reclaimed hickory**
Restoration Timber, San
Francisco, CA
**Graphics** Amy Fritz, San
Francisco, CA
**General contractor** Ben
Davies, San Francisco, CA

## PLUK

Grote Houtstraat 150
2011 SX Haarlem
Netherlands
www.plukmij.nl/
**Design** Tjep.
**Project team** Frank Tjepkema,
Janneke Hooymans, Tina
Stieger, Leonie Janssen,
Marloes Pronk, Bertrand
Gravier, Camille Cortet
www.tjep.com

## PROEF

Gossalklaan 12
1014 DC Amsterdam
Netherlands
www.proefamsterdam.nl
**Design** Studio Marije
Vogelzang
www.marijevogelzang.nl

## REPUBLICA CAFÉ

Alameda de Hércules, 27
41002 Seville
Spain
www.republicacafe.com
**Design** Ernesto de Ceano, DCD
Interiorismo
www.dcdinteriorismo.com

## RESTAURANT 51

51, Rue de Bercy
75002 Paris
France
www.cinematheque.fr
**Design** John Mascaro and
Eléonore Morand – Mut-
Architecture
www.Mut-Architecture.com
together with Brigitte Bouillot
and Benoit Millot – Le Potager
Design
www.lepotagerdesigncom
**Table** Jürg Bader, Kunstbetrieb
www.kunstbetrieb.ch

## RONO ICE CREAM

Akaike, Nisshin
Aichi Prefecture 470-0125
Japan
www.rono.jp
**Design** Hiroyuki Miyake
www.hiroyukimiyake.com

## THE ROYAL CAFÉ

Amagertorv 6
1160 Copenhagen
Denmark
www.theroyalcafe.dk
**Interior design** Rud
Christiansen and Lo
Østergaard

## SILVER CAFÉ

Marine Road West
Morecambe LA3 1BS
UK
**Design** Arca
www.arca.co.uk

## SNOG

9 Brewer Street
London W1F ORG
UK
www.ifancyasnog.com
**Architecture and lighting
design** Cinimod Studio
**Branding and graphics** Ico
Design
**Main contractor** Vivid Interiors
**Digital lighting installation**
E-Luminate
**Architectural lighting**
Deltalight
**Bespoke feature globe
lighting** Cinimod Studio
**Signage and light boxes** The
Lettering Centre
**Audio system** Inspired
Dwellings

## SWEETGREEN

4831 Bethesda Ave
Bethesda, MD 20814
USA
www.sweetgreen.com
**Client** Greens Restaurant
Group
**Architect** Core Architecture
+ Design, Peter F. Hapstak,
Project Principal; Sabrina
Cheung, Project Architect
www.coredc.com
**Graphics** Unison
www.unisonagency.com
**Recycled wood furniture**
Counterevolution
www.counterevolutionnyc.
com
**Floor tiles** Daltile Concrete
Connections

## TANGYSWEET

2029 P St NW
Washington, DC 20036
USA
www.tangysweet.com
**Design** KUBE architecture
www.kube-arch.com
**Lightboxes** Lightblocks®
**Lighting consultants** George
Sexton Associates
**Lighting installation**
ColorKinetics
**Contractor** Construction
Commercial, Inc.
**Steelwork** Metal Specialities
**Woodwork** Andrew
Christenberry

## WAKU-WAKU

Schauenburgerstraße 55
20095 Hamburg
Germany
www.waku-waku.eu
**Design** Ippolito Fleitz Group
GmbH
www.ifgroup.org
**Team** Peter Ippolito, Gunter
Fleitz, Alexander Fehre,
Sherief Sabet, Silke Schreier,
Ting Xiu
**Artwork** Monica Trenkler
**Lighting design** Pfarré
Lighting Design, München
**Branding** Pajama, London

# INDEX

Page numbers in *italics* refer to picture captions

## A

Ab Rogers Design 162–5
Africa
    Royal Restaurant, Dar es Salaam, Tanzania *21*
Alameda de Hércules, Seville, Spain 58
Alison Brooks Architects 53
American diners *11*, 15–16, *81*, 163
    St Paul, Minnesota *19*
    Willow Grove Diner, Pennsylvania *15*
Ando, Koichi (Ando Gallery) 221
Ant chair (Jacobsen) 32, *34*
Arca 70–5
Architecture and Hygiene 63
Art Basel Miami Beach 63
Artisan du Chocolat, London, UK 230–5
Asylum
    Chocolate Research Facility, Singapore 242–7
    Frolick, Singapore 124–9
Atelier Archange 150–5
Australia
    Fish 349, Hobart, Tasmania 196–201
Austria
    Café Hawelka, Vienna *11*
    Café Schwarzenberg, Vienna *11*
    coffee houses, Vienna 15
Avanzi, Philippe (Atelier Archange) 150–5

## B

badges 125, *127, 129*
Baines, Rob (Snog) 137
Bang & Olufsen 32
Bangalore Express, London, UK *21*
bentos (lunch boxes) *10, 237*
Bernoulli, Hans Benno 156
Bertoia, Harry *83*

Bilbao, Spain 25
Bloom in the Park, Malmö, Sweden 180–5
Bloomberg, Janet (Kube Architects) 131–2
Blossom, Nagano, Japan 214–17
Blumenthal, Heston 163, 164
Boolean (Tokyo University Tetsumon Café), Tokyo, Japan 192–5
Boon, Irma 103, 104
brands and branding
    cafés 63
    confectionery restaurants 221–2, 243
    Japanese-influenced restaurants 116, 119
    pasta restaurants 103
    restaurants 151, 163, 164, *173, 174, 178, 187*
    yoghurt bars 124–5, *137*
Bretillot, Marc 16
brgr, New York, USA 202–7
Bunny Lane, New Jersey, USA 63
burger bars 10, 11, 12
    brgr, New York, USA 202–7
    Pop Burger, New York, USA 16, *79*
    *see also* McDonald's

## C

Café Hawelka, Vienna, Austria *11*
Café Schwarzenberg, Vienna, Austria *11*
cafeterias 19
    Boolean, Tokyo University, Japan 192–5
    Espresso *K, Delft University, Netherlands 42–5
    Kirschgarten Cafeteria, Basel, Switzerland 156–61
Caffé Florian, Piazza San Marco, Venice, Italy 10, *11*
Camper FoodBALL, Barcelona, Spain 16, 19, 38, *172–5*
Camper shoe chain *173*

Candy Restaurant, Tokyo, Japan 236–41
Carlsberg Group 32
La Casa Azul, Valencia, Spain 96–101
Cathedral Group 53
CCS Architecture 66–9
Ceano, Ernesto de 58–61
La Cerámica Valenciana 98
Cha Cha Moon, London, UK 19, 108–13
China: street café, Hangzhou *10*
Christiansen, Rud 30–5
Cinémathèque Française, Paris, France 167
Cinimod Studio 136–41
Ciscar, Herme 96–101
coffee houses 10, 12, 15
    in Constantinople (painting by Preziosi) *13*
    'Eagle's Nest' (Kehlsteinhaus), Berchtesgaden, Germany *16*
    in Vienna, Austria 15
    *see also* espresso bars
Collins, David (David Collins Studio) 47
Constantinople coffee house (painting by Preziosi) *13*
Core 186–91
Coso Café, Palermo, Sicily 36–41
Counterevolution 187
cultural aspects 10, 12, 15, 31–2, 86, *87*

## D

David Collins Studio 46–51
DCD Interiorismo 58–61
delicatessens 67
Denmark
    Kafferiet, Copenhagen 31
    The Royal Café, Copenhagen 30–5
Deptford, London, UK 53, 54
The Deptford Project, London, UK 52–7
2chevaux stools (Lens) 234

Dorte Mandrup Arkitekter 31
Droog 209, *210*

## E

'Eagle's Nest' (Kehlsteinhaus), Berchtesgaden, Germany *16*
Eames, Charles and Ray 151, *245*
East Beach Café, Littlehampton, Sussex, UK 24–9
'eating design' 20, 208–13
espresso bars 10
    Espresso *K, Delft, Netherlands 42–5
    illy Push Button Café, Venice, Italy 62–5
    Espresso *K, Delft, Netherlands 42–5
    Estado Puro, Madrid, Spain 84–9

## F

fast food 10–11, 16, 20, 115, 118, 150, *177*
*Fast Food: Roadside Restaurants in the Automobile Age* (Jakle and Sculle) 19
*Fast Food Nation* (Schlosser) 12
fast food outlets 11–12, 15–16, 19
    Camper FoodBALL, Barcelona, Spain 16, 19, 38, *172–5*
    Itsu, London, UK 118–21
    Julia's Pasta, Amsterdam, Netherlands 102–5
    Pizza Bar, New York, USA 16, *78–83*
    Pop Burger, New York, USA 16, *79*
    Waku-Waku, Hamburg, Germany 114–17
    *see also* McDonald's
Fish 349, Hobart, Tasmania, Australia 196–201
fish and chip shops 10, 15

Blackpool, Lancashire, UK
15
food design 16, 19, 20, 31,
173, 202, 236–7 see also
'eating design'
France
Cinémathèque Française,
Paris 167
McDonald's, Paris 155
Restaurant 51, Paris
166–71
Fritz Hansen 32, 34, 151
Frolick, Singapore 124–9

**G**
Galeano, Mauricio (James &
Mau) 85
García, Mónica 96–101
Gasbarro, Ornella 36–41
Gaztelu, Jaime (James &
Mau) 85
Gehry, Frank 25, 167, 171
Geno's Steak restaurant,
Philadelphia, USA 11
Georg Jensen 32
George Sexton Associates 132
Germany
'Eagle's Nest'
(Kehlsteinhaus),
Berchtesgaden 16
Waku-Waku, Hamburg
114–17
Gonzalez Correa, Adolfo 98, 99
Good Restaurants AG 115
Gordon, Aaron (TangySweet)
131
Grace, Vicente (La Casa Azul)
97
graphics 10, 16
cafés 58, 72
confectionery restaurants
221, 222, 226, 234, 237,
246
fast food restaurants 10,
12, 16, 151, 173, 174, 177,
178, 179
Japanese-influenced
restaurants 116, 119
pizza and tapas bars 78, 86
restaurants 163, 164, 169,

171, 196–7, 199
yoghurt bars 124, 125,
132, 138
groovisions 221, 222
Guelke, Matthew (The Plant
Café Organic) 67
Guggenheim Museum, Bilbao,
Spain 25
Guixé, Martí
Camper FoodBALL,
Barcelona, Spain 16, 19,
38, 172–5
Candy Restaurant, Tokyo,
Japan 236–41
Guyé, Isabelle (McDonald's
European Restaurant
Development and Design
Studio) 150, 151

**H**
Hafod Eryri, Snowdon, Wales
16
Hakkasan, London, UK 109
Happy stools (Pedrali) 178
Hapstak, Peter (Core) 186–7
Harris, Dominic (Cinimod
Studio) 137, 138
Hayon, Jaime 85
health food outlets
The Plant Café Organic, San
Francisco, USA 66–9
Pluk, Haarlem, Netherlands
176–9
Sweetgreen, Bethesda,
Maryland, USA 186–91
Heatherwick, Thomas
(Thomas Heatherwick
Studio) 25, 26
HHF Architects 156–61
Hobart, Tasmania, Australia
196
Holley, Marc (Silver
Restaurant) 72
Holmegaard Glass 32
Hopper, Edward 10

**I**
ice cream parlours 20
Rono Ice Cream, Aichi,
Japan 142–7

Ico Design 136–41
illy coffee 63
illy Push Button Café, Venice,
Italy 62–5
Ippolito Fleitz Group 114–17
Iran: tea rooms, Vakil Bazaar,
Shiraz 13
Ireland: John Street Tea and
Wine, Kilkenny 46–51
Isetan Department Store,
Shinjuku, Japan 222
Italy
Caffé Florian, Piazza San
Marco, Venice 10
Coso Café, Palermo, Sicily
36–41
illy Push Button Café,
Venice 62–5
Pizza Perez, Syracuse,
Sicily 38, 90–5
Itsu, London, UK 118–21

**J**
Jacobsen, Arne 32, 34, 151
James & Mau 84–9
Jammet, Nicolas
(Sweetgreen) 186, 187
Japan
Blossom, Nagano 214–17
Boolean (Tokyo University
Tetsumon Café), Tokyo
192–5
Candy Restaurant, Tokyo
236–41
Isetan Department Store,
Shinjuku 222
100%ChocolateCafé, Tokyo
220–3
Rono Ice Cream, Aichi
142–7
John Street Tea and Wine,
Kilkenny, Ireland 46–51
Julia's Pasta, Amsterdam,
Netherlands 102–5

**K**
Kafferiet, Copenhagen,
Denmark 31
Kalkin, Adam (Architecture
and Hygiene) 62–5

Kamuro, Shinya (Torafu
Architects) 192
Kara's Cupcakes, San
Francisco, USA 224–9
Kehlsteinhaus ('Eagle's
Nest'), Berchtesgaden,
Germany 16
Kengo Kuma & Associates 19,
108–13
Kilkenny, Ireland 47
Kirschgarten Cafeteria, Basel,
Switzerland 156–61
Krassa, Afroditi 118–21
Kube Architecture 130–5
Kuma, Kengo (Kengo Kuma &
Associates) 19, 109–10
Kunstbetrieb 171
Kvadrat 32

**L**
Lacroix, André (Waku-Waku)
115
Le Pellec, Pascal (Waku-Waku)
115
Le Potager Design 166–71
Lee, Chris (Asylum) 124–5,
243
Lee, John (Arca) 71–2
Lens, Bart (LENS°ASS
Architecten) 231
LENS°ASS Architecten 230–5
Lewis, Mark (The Plant Café
Organic) 67
Liaigre, Christian 109
Liebenthal, Roy (Pop Burger
and Pizza Bar) 79
Lind, Michael (Montalba
Architects) 225
Lindvall, Jonas (Lindvall
A&D) 181
Lindvall A&D 180–5
Little Chef chain 16
Kettering,
Northamptonshire, UK
162–5
Popham, Hampshire, UK
163
Littlehampton, Sussex, UK
25–6
Litvinenko, Alexander 118

Locker, Bianca 116
Ingns 32, 104, 110, 113, 174, 197, 202, 237
La Lonja de la Seda, Valencia, Spain 97, 100
Lui chairs (Lindvall for Skandiform) 182, 185

## M

Mahou beer 86–7, 89
Malone, Jim (Counterevolution) 187
Marks & Spencer 20
Masamichi, Katayama (Wonderwall) 221
Mascaro, John (Mut-Architecture) 167, 171
McDonald, Richard and Maurice 12
McDonald's 11, 12, 150
    in Europe 16, 150–5
    Holborn, London, UK 151
    Lexington, Kentucky 12
    Moscow, Russia 10, 15
    Paris, France 155
Meiji confectionery 221
Merkx+Girod 102–5
Metcalfe, Julian (Itsu chain) 118
Miyake, Hiroyuki 142–7
Moncada, Francesco
    Coso Café, Palermo, Sicily 36–41
    Pizza Perez, Syracuse, Sicily 38, 90–5
Montalba, David (Montalba Architects) 225, 226
Montalba Architects, Inc. 224–9
Morant, Eléonore (Mut-Architecture) 167
Moreamore (graffiti artist) 59, 61
Morecambe, Lancashire 71
Morgan, Luke 54
Murray, Sophie 26
Mut-Architecture 166–71
Myerscough, Morag (Studio Myerscough) 53, 54

## N

Nakamura, Ryuji 214–17
Neman, Jonathan (Sweetgreen) 186
Netherlands
    Espresso *K, Delft 42–5
    Julia's Pasta, Amsterdam 102–5
    Picknick, Rotterdam 210
    Pluk, Haarlem 16, 176–9
    Proef Amsterdam 208–13
    Proef Rotterdam 210
noodle bars: Cha Cha Moon, London, UK 19, 108–13

## O

100%ChocolateCafé, Tokyo, Japan 220–3
Østergaard, Lo 30–5
Outline 21

## P

packaging 67, 119, 121, 125, 187, 221, 222, 243, 246
Pajama 115, 116
Parr, Martin 10, 12
pasta restaurants: Julia's Pasta, Amsterdam, Netherlands 102–5
Patijn, Wytze (Dean of Faculty of Architecture, Delft University) 44
Pawson, John 109
Perez, Vicenzo (Pizza Perez) 91
Picknick, Rotterdam, Netherlands 210
Piketty, Hughes (Restaurant 51) 167
Pizza Bar, New York, USA 16, 78–83
Pizza Perez, Syracuse, Sicily 38, 90–5
pizzerias
    Pizza Bar, New York, USA 16, 78–83
    Pizza Perez, Syracuse, Sicily 38, 90–5
The Plant Café Organic, San Francisco, USA 66–9

Pluk, Haarlem, Netherlands 16, 176–9
Point Supreme 91, 93, 95
Pop Burger, New York, USA 16, 79
Praline 164
Pret A Manger 20, 118
Preziosi, Amadeo: coffee house in Constantinople 13
Proef Amsterdam, Netherlands 208–13
Proef Rotterdam, Netherlands 210
push button houses (Kalkin) 63

## Q

Quik House (Kalkin) 63

## R

railway carriages as eating places 15, 53, 54
Rawlings, Simon (David Collins Studio) 47, 48
Ray Hole Architects 16
recycling 42, 43, 44, 54, 56, 119, 187, 189
República Café, Alameda de Hércules, Seville, Spain 58–61
Restaurant 51, Paris, France 166–71
retro design 11–12, 16, 80, 81, 138, 164, 165, 246
Ritt, Jon (Montalba Architects) 225
Robson, Dominic 164
Rockwell Group 202–7
Rogers, Ab (Ab Rogers Design) 16, 163–4, 165
Rogers, Richard 53
Roncero, Paco 85, 86
Rono Ice Cream, Aichi, Japan 142–7
The Royal Café, Copenhagen, Denmark 30–5
Royal Copenhagen porcelain 31, 32
Royal Restaurant, Dar es Salaam, Tanzania, Africa 21

Ru, Nathaniel (Sweetgreen) 186
Russell, Chris (brgr) 202
Russia: McDonald's, Moscow 10, 15
Russo, Giovanni 79, 83

## S

Sake No Hana, London, UK 19, 110
San Francisco, USA 67
sandwiches 20, 31
school cafeterias see university and school cafeterias
Seleko (graffiti artist) 59, 61
Servex BV 103
Shitake stool (Wanders for Moroso) 138
Shokado bento (lunch box) 10
Silver Café, Morecambe, Lancashire, UK 70–5
Singapore
    Chocolate Research Facility 242–7
    Frolick 124–9
'smushi' (sandwiches) 31
Snog, London, UK 19, 136–41
The Soda Fountain magazine 19–20
soda fountains 19
Spain
    Camper FoodBALL, Barcelona 16, 19, 38, 172–5
    La Casa Azul, Valencia 96–101
    Estado Puro, Madrid 84–9
    Guggenheim Museum, Bilbao 25
    La Lonja de la Seda, Valencia 97, 100
    República Café, Alameda de Hércules, Seville 58–61
    La Terraza del Casino, Madrid 85
street café, Hangzhou, China 10
Studio Myerscough 52–7
sushi 19, 121

sushi restaurants: Sake No
Hana, London, UK *19,* 110
sustainability issues 16, 54,
115, 116, 150, 151, 174,
186, 187
Suzuno, Koichi (Torafu
Architects) 192
Sweden: Bloom in the Park,
Malmö 180–5
Sweetgreen, Bethesda,
Maryland, USA 186–91
Switzerland: Kirschgarten
Cafeteria, Basel 156–61
Syracuse, Sicily 91

**T**

TangySweet, Washington, DC,
USA 19, 130–5
tapas bars: Estado Puro,
Madrid, Spain 84–9
Taste Festival, Hobart,
Tasmania, Australia 196
Tayar, Ali (Parallel Design) 16,
78–83
Tcherevkoff, Sasha (Pop
Burger and Pizza Bar) 79
tea rooms 47
John Street Tea and Wine,
Kilkenny, Ireland 46–51
Vakil Bazaar, Shiraz, Iran *13*
Tepedino, Massimo 36–41
La Terraza del Casino, Madrid,
Spain 85
Terroir 196–201
Thomas Heatherwick Studio
24–9
Tjep. 176–9
Tjepkema, Frank (Tjep.) 16,
177
Torafu Architects 192–5
2012 Architecten 42–5

**U**

UK
Artisan du Chocolat,
London 230–5
Bangalore Express, London
*21*
Cha Cha Moon, London 19,
108–13

The Deptford Project,
London 52–7
East Beach Café,
Littlehampton, Sussex
24–9
fish and chip shop,
Blackpool, Lancashire *15*
Hakkasan, London 109
Itsu, London 118–21
Little Chef, Kettering,
Northamptonshire 162–5
Little Chef, Popham,
Hampshire 163
McDonald's, Holborn,
London *151*
Sake No Hana, London
*19,* 110
Silver Café, Morecambe,
Lancashire 70–5
Snog, London 19, 136–41
Wagamama, London 109
*see also* Wales
Unison 187
university and school
cafeterias
Boolean, Tokyo University,
Japan 192–5
Espresso *K, Delft
University, Netherlands
42–5
Kirschgarten Cafeteria,
Basel, Switzerland 156–61
Uribe, Pablo (Snog) 137
USA
brgr, New York 202–7
Bunny Lane, New Jersey
63
diner, St Paul, Minnesota *19*
Geno's Steak restaurant,
Philadelphia *11*
Kara's Cupcakes, San
Francisco 224–9
McDonald's, Lexington,
Kentucky *12*
Pizza Bar, New York 16,
78–83
The Plant Café Organic, San
Francisco 66–9
Pop Burger, New York
16, 79

Sweetgreen, Bethesda,
Maryland 186–91
TangySweet, Washington,
DC 19, 130–5
Willow Grove Diner,
Pennsylvania *15*

**V**

Venice Biennale (2007) 63
Vidal, Igi (Bloom in the Park)
181
*vinotecas* (wine bars): La
Casa Azul, Valencia, Spain
96–101
Vogelzang, Marije 20, 208–13

**W**

Wagamama, London, UK 109
Waku-Waku, Hamburg,
Germany 114–17
Wales: Hafod Eryri, Snowdon
*16*
Wanders, Marcel 138
Weeks, David 48
Wiederkehr, Gido 157, *158*
Willow Grove Diner,
Pennsylvania, USA *15*
Wimpy 163
wine bars: La Casa Azul,
Valencia, Spain 96–101
Wolff Olins 118
Wöltje, Gregor (Waku-Waku)
115
Wonderwall 220–3
Wood, Jane 26

**X**

XXXL lamp (Lens) *232, 234*

**Y**

Yau, Alan *19,* 109
yoghurt bars
Frolick, Singapore 124–9
Snog, London, 19, 136–41
TangySweet, Washington,
DC, USA 19, 130–5
Young Creatives Network 138

**Z**

Zwierzynska, Agata 103, 104

# PHOTO CREDITS

6 © Corbis

8 © Arne Hodalic/CORBIS

9 © Martin Parr/MAGNUM PHOTOS

10 top © Studio Eye/CORBIS

10 bottom © Yang Liu/CORBIS

11 top Creative Commons: j.reed/flickr

11 bottom Imagno/Getty Images

12 left Creative Commons: Pink Sherbet Photography/flickr

12 right © William A. Bake/CORBIS

13 top © Diego Lezama Orezzoli/CORBIS

13 bottom © Stapleton Collection/CORBIS

14 Peter Adams/Getty Images

15 © Lake County Museum/CORBIS

16 © Peter Kneffel/epa/CORBIS

17 Courtesy of Ray Hole Architects

18 Courtesy of Hakkasan Limited

19 © Minnesota Historical Society/CORBIS

20 Photo Philip Vile, courtesy of Outline

21 Christopher Pillitz/Getty Images

22 Timothy Soar

24–5 Nathan Willock/VIEW

27 Andy Stagg/VIEW

28 Andy Stagg/VIEW

29 top left and bottom left Andy Stagg/VIEW

29 right Julian Abrams/VIEW

30–35 Courtesy of The Royal Café

36–41 Alberto Moncada

42–45 Photos: Karola van Rooyen/2012 Architecten

46–51 Mark Scott Photography

52–57 Richard Learoyd

58–61 Courtesy DCD Interiorismo

62–65 Luca Campigotto

66–69 Cesar Rubio, San Francisco, CA and Javier Haddad, New York, NY

70–75 Timothy Soar

76 Javier Peñas

78–83 © Joshua McHugh

84–89 Javier Peñas

90–95 Alberto Moncada

96–101 Manuel Sanchez

102–105 © Roos Aldershoff Fotografie

106 © Zooey Braun FOTOGRAFIE

108 Courtesy of the author

109–113 Courtesy of Hakkasan

114–117 © Zooey Braun FOTOGRAFIE

118–121 Courtesy of Itsu

122 Ricoh Adachi

124–129 Courtesy of Asylum

130–135 PAUL BURK PHOTOGRAPHY

136–141 Courtesy of Cinimod Studio and Snog

142–147 Ricoh Adachi

148 Tom Bisig, Basel/Switzerland

150–155 Courtesy of McDonald's

156–161 Tom Bisig, Basel/Switzerland

162–165 John Short/Little Chef

166–171 Brigitte Bouillot

172–175 © Knölke/Imagekontainer

176–179 Courtesy of Tjep.

180–185 Johan Kalén

186–191 © Michael Moran Photography

192–195 Daici Ano

196–201 © Jonathan Wherrett and Brett Boardman Photography

202–207 Courtesy of Rockwell Group

208–213 Courtesy of Studio Marije Vogelzang

214–217 Courtesy of Ryuji Nakamura

218 © Mitch Tobias

220–223 Kozo Takayama

224–229 © Mitch Tobias

230–235 © Artisan du Chocolat www.artisanduchocolat.com/ Photographer: Laurie Fletcher

236–241 © Knölke/Imagekontainer

242–247 Courtesy of Asylum

# AUTHOR ACKNOWLEDGEMENTS

I would like to thank warmly the many designers and architects who took the time to discuss the projects in this book and share images of their work. Working with the team at Laurence King – Philip Cooper and Gaynor Sermon – has been a pleasure, and I'm very grateful to Adam Hooper for making the book look so nice. But above all, thanks to Gioia, Sashy and Trish for their support.